AF652149

CHANGING GENDER EQUATION
WITH SPECIAL REFERENCE TO NAGALAND

CHANGING GENDER EQUATION

WITH SPECIAL REFERENCE TO NAGALAND

Edited by
Kedilezo Kikhi
Narola Dangti Kikhi

AKANSHA PUBLISHING HOUSE
NEW DELHI - 110002 (INDIA)

AKANSHA PUBLISHING HOUSE
4649-B,Ansari Road,
Daryaganj, New Dellii-11 0002
Phones:23268193, 9811582579, 09435116718
Email: ektabooks@yahoo.com
visit us: www.akanshapublishinghouse.com

Changing Gender Equation with Special Reference to Nagaland

© Authors

First Published 2009

ISBN 978-81-8370-185-3

[All rights reserved. No part of this publication may be reproduced or transmitted, in any form or by any means, without prior permission of the editors. Any person who does any unauthorised act in relation to this publication may be liable to criminal prosecution and civil claims for damages.]

PRINTED IN INDIA

Published by Akansha Publishing House, New Delhi-110002 and printed at Capital Offset Press, Delhi.

Contents

Foreword

The study of the status and role of women has assumed a central place in the social science discourse in the country today. The early social historians had primarily included certain women issues in their narration of social reform movements of the nineteenth century. Their emphasis was mainly on the oppressive condition of women that was reflected in the social practices such as child marriage, polygyny, prohibition of widow remarriage, sati, purdah system and so on. These issues were highlighted to focus the need of undertaking welfare measures for ameliorating the socio-economic condition of womenfolk. This process of academic de bate and discussion which was initiated in the nineteenth century took a different shape in the early phase of the twentieth century when the nationalist leaders began to voice their concern not only with regard to the degrading status of women but also on the issue of structured gender inequality involved in the patriarchal family system in different parts of the country. Mahatma Gandhi, the tallest of all the nationalist political leaders adopted an entirely new approach to focus on the social and legal disabilities imposed on women in matters of guardianship, inheritance and marriage.

A new phase, however, started in the study of women question after the independence. Though the situation was not so encouraging immediately after the Independence, the year 1975 became a catalyst as the publication in 1974 of the Parliamentary Commission on the Status of Women Report stirred the conscience of the nation. The Report initiated the process of rethinking on the question of gender disparity. Thus a paradigm shift came about in the understanding of the status and role of women. The intermingling of patriarchy with demeaning position of women has produced a highly iniquitous and discriminatory social system. That being the case, the national social policy has been re-oriented in the direction of gender equality with a transition from the policy of women "welfare" to women "empowerment". Such a transformation in the nature and quality of policy intervention has had also a direct bearing on the thinking and corresponding agenda of the social scientists in general and sociologists in particular. Consequently, a large number of gender related studies are undertaken highlighting all crucial dimensions involved in women's life - social oppression, cultural exclusion and economic deprivation.

The present volume meticulously prepared by the two young Naga scholars is also in line with the same trend. The collection of essays contributed by the cross -sections of professional sociologists, journalists, administrators and a few young researchers provides a panoramic view of the changing gender equation in Naga society. Dr. Kedilezo Kikhi and Mrs. Narola Dangti Kikhi has competently performed the task of bringing more than a dozen articles together dealing with some of the major issues associated with women in one of the dominant communities located in the northeastern corner of India. Globalization and empowerment, changing gender equity and status achievement, inheritance and economic role of women, the emerging trends towards political participation are some key themes discussed in these essays. In addition to the diversity of themes, the studies included here cover the situation prevailing among half a dozen Naga communities located in different regions of Nagaland. The study thus provides with fairly a good insight into the values, and gender seems to be only a politically correct stance we talk at meetings and discussions. Gender disparities still abound. We have 'come a long way', but we have only made progress toward changing the situation rather than eradicating it. We are hopeful this edition will be a beneficial reading for all the sections of people in Nagaland and elsewhere.

14th Jan. 2009 *Prof. M.N. Karna*

Acknowledgements

We take this opportunity to acknowledge the active and inspiring participation of all the learned resource persons as well as those who contributed papers in absentia - coming from a cross section of academia, journalists, administrators and young scholars in this ICSSR NERC sponsored seminar on "The Changing Gender Equation", the outcome of which is the publication of this volume.

We are grateful to Dr. C.J. Thomas, Director ICSSR NERC, Shillong and his staff for assisting and sponsoring the seminar. We are also thankful to the Principal and the staff of Sazolie College, Jotsoma. Our colleagues, Ms. Theyieseno Keditsu and Mr. Noketho Rhetso, Department of English, Sazolie College, deserve a special mention for being the backbones right from the beginning till the end. They have played a major role for the success of the seminar.

Gender inequality is a problem of mindsets and attitudes. Patriarchy influences the worldview of women as much as it does that of men. Hence women themselves resist change unless they are trained to think out of the box of patriarchy. Naga society is steeped in patriarchal values, and gender seems to be only a politically correct stance we talk at meetings and discussions. Gender disparities still abound. We have 'come a long way', but we have only made progress toward changing the situation rather than eradicating it. We are hopeful this edition will be a beneficial reading for all the sections of people in Nagaland and elsewhere.

Prof. M.N. Karna deserves special thanks for agreeing to write the foreword. Lastly we appreciate M.P. Misra, Akansha Publishing House, New Delhi for having agreed to undertake this publication work.

Kedilezo Kikhi
Narola Dangti Kikhi

Our Contributors

1. **Mrs. Monalisa Changkija**
Editor, Nagaland Page, Dimapur, Nagaland.

2. **Mr. Viraho Hibo**
Vice Principal & HoD, Dept. of Education, Japfü Christian College, Kigwema.

3. **Mr. Chandan Debnath**
Lecturer, Dimapur Govt. College & Research Scholar, Dept. of Business Administration, Tezpur University, Assam.

4. **Mr. Amiya Kumar Das**
Guest Lecturer, Dept. of Sociology, Tezpur University & Research Scholar, JNU, New Delhi.

5. **Mr. Arjun Das**
Research Scholar, Department of History, North Bengal University.

6. **Mrs. Visakhonü Hibo**
Lecturer, Dept. of Sociology, Japfü Christian College, Kigwema & Research Scholar, Nagaland University.

7. **Mr. M. Temjen Longkumer**
Lecturer, Department of Sociology, Alder college, Kohima & Research Scholar, Department of Sociology, Nagaland University.

8. **Mr. Athungo Ovung**
Lecturer, Tribal Research Centre, Nagaland University & Research Scholar, Department of Sociology, Nagaland University.

9. **Dr. Christina Kekhrieseno**
Lecturer, Department of Sociology, Wankhao (Govt.) College, Mon.

10. **Dr. Koseno**
NGO Coordinator, Nagaland Aids Control Society, Government of Nagaland.

11. **Ms. Elizabeth Vithazonu**
    Lady Mobilizer, National Cooperative Education Field Project, Kohima & Research Scholar, Dept. of Sociology, Nagaland University.

12. **Mr. Lichumo Enie**
    Lecturer, Department of History, Japfü Christian College, Kigwema.

13. **Mr. N.S. Khaikho**
    Research Scholar, Department of Sociology, Nagaland University.

14. **Mrs. Narola Dangti**
    Lecturer, Department of English, Sazolie College, Jotsoma & Research Scholar, Department of English, Nagaland University.

15. **Dr. Kedilezo Kikhi**
    Lecturer, Department of Sociology, Nagaland University.

1

Changing Gender Equation: Compared Cross-Culturally

Kedilezo Kikhi & Narola Dangti Kikhi

[Gender encompasses the socially constructed roles of women and men. Throughout the world, the use of gender to ascribe status for years has perpetuated a system of gender role and gender inequality. But ever since women have become aware of alternatives to the existing system, they have worked tirelessly for changes in the status quo. No longer will most children grow to be fifteen and not have met a female pilot or a female taxi driver. We have 'come a long way', but we have only made progress towards changing the situation rather than eradicating it. Women must reach parity with men in all the major areas of life: politics, economics and education. This paper calls attention to a concept of institutional discrimination, on how people are socialized into gender roles?]

I

Population experts, applying standard formulas for sex ratios at birth and across the life course, have discovered that there are at least 100 million fewer females than there would be if boys and girls received similar nutrition and health care (Sen, 1990; United Nations, 1993).

It has been reported that China and India account for almost two-thirds of the missing children and adults. These are both societies with a long tradition of valuing males more highly than females; the birth of a son is greeted with great joy; that of a daughter with sadness. But it has always been thus, so what can account for the sudden recent shortage of females? Quite simply, the ultrasound scanner, which can identify the sex of a foetus. (Hess, Markson & Stein, 2000).

In China, the government's effort to control population growth has emphasized the ideal of one child per couple. Because the family's preferred child is a boy, girl babies often contract a fatal illness or simply vanish, allowing the couple to try again for a son. And many girls are never born. Whereas the typical sex ratio at birth is 104/5 boys for every 100 girls, the ratio was close to 120/100 as ultrasound technology spread throughout China until sex screening was banned in 1995.

In China, those who have babies in violation of the restrictions are punished with heavy fines. However, Zhang Weiqing, Director of the National Population and Family Planning Commission, reports a new trend where China's wealthy are showing disdain for the policy by paying to have as many children as they wanted. It also reports "the number of rich people and celebrities having more than one child is on a rapid increase, and nearly 10 per cent of them even have three." (*The Times of India*, May 8, 2007).

In parts of India, the low cultural value placed on females is reinforced by their even-lower economic worth. A daughter is a financial disaster, producing little and needing a dowry to marry. Thanks to the low-cost ultrasound machine, Indian physicians do a brisk business in sex determination tests, followed by the termination of almost all pregnancies involving a female foetus. For families without access to ultrasound, daughters typically receive much less food and health care than sons do, with consequently higher death rates throughout childhood. The only variable that increases the survival chances of a daughter is living in an area dependent on rice cultivation, where women play an important role. (Kishor, 1993)

Throughout the world, systems of social stratification are gendered, that is, they are based on a differential evaluation of males and females. The result of this gendered inequality is that, in all but a very few societies, power, prestige, and property are unequally distributed on the basis of sex. It is a cultural universal that where men and women know and do different things, men's work and wisdom is more highly valued than that of women. Sex is also a prime determinant of a person's location in other hierarchies, such as those based on religion, race, ethnicity, and age as well as education, occupation, and income.

II

Sex refers to the biological differences between males and females. The genetic differences between males and females are straightforward. Each ovum (egg) the female produces has an X chromosome. Each sperm from the male carries either an X chromosome or a Y chromosome. When the ovum is fertilized with a sperm, the resulting new cell will have, then one X from the female, and either an X or a Y from the male. Two X chromosomes produce a girl, and an X and a Y produce a boy. When the embryo is three weeks old, some organs develop male characteristics and some develop female characteristics, due to secretion of testosterone caused by the Y chromosome.

Every society socializes its males and females to behaviour that is considered 'masculine' or 'feminine' within that culture. The term gender refers to culturally transmitted differences between men and women. We learn gender-appropriate behaviour through role-modeling, explicit instruction, and cultural transmission, just as we learn other social behaviours. Thus gender refers to the social rather than biological characteristics that are related to being male or female (Wallace & Wallace, 1989).

- *Sex refers to biological characteristics while gender refers to social or cultural characteristics. Gender is learned.*

The theme in this article calls attention to a concept of institutional discrimination. Legal discrimination is, after all, illegal. Presumably, if one can document legal discrimination, one can remove such discrimination through the courts or legislatures. Institutional discrimination, on the other hand, is much more insidious and, therefore, more difficult to rectify.

Institutional discrimination resides within the fabric of society. Harrington (1984) poetically called institutional discrimination 'structures of misery'. Eitzen and Baca-Zinn (1994) describe institutional discrimination as "the customary ways of doing things, prevailing attitudes and expectations, and accepted structural arrangements [that] works to the disadvantage [of the poor]." Institutional discrimination explains much inequality in gender (and race and ethnicity) found in the workplace.

III

Perspectives

"Few areas of science are as littered with intellectual rubbish as the study of innate ... differences of wishful thinking." (Reinharz, 1986). In each case, also the reported differences are far smaller than the similarities between women and men. (Bem, 1993). But the search goes on, and interest in the topic never fades. One of the most current researches, however, actually reinforces many insights of the sociological perspectives: (1) our species is enormously adaptable; (2) any effects of brain structure are subject to modification by experience; and (3) behaviour is the outcome of complex interactions between the organism and the social and physical environment.

Arguments that explain male superiority by reference to men's greater body size and aggressiveness are the least persuasive. Size is not necessarily associated with intelligence, and highly aggressive individuals are usually labeled dangerous and are locked up. Regarding hormones, most research finds only a weak link between hormone levels and specific behaviour, and the cause-and-effect is unclear; in many cases, hormone levels rise after a contest is won.

As for the evolutionary argument that human behaviour is an extension of earlier primate adaptations, the evidence suggests wide variability among species in patterns of cooperation and competition between the sexes. In fact, the study reveals that among chimpanzees, our close primate ancestors, aggression in males and submissiveness in female appears less frequently than among most other species.

From a sociological perspective, it is most useful to see sex differences as rooted in social experience rather than being fixed in our genes, hormones, or evolutionary past. For example, social psychologists suggest that because women nurture infants and raise children, they tend to develop a strong sense of connectedness to others. Males, in contrast, who must separate from the mother to become fully masculine, tend to be detached from other people; the closer the original attachment, the more violent the rejection (Gilmore, 1990). In this view, such early experiences produce girls and women fearful of commitment—not the best recipe for fulfilling adult relationships.

Sociologists generally agree that women and men fit their gender roles largely because they are socialized to do so. However, they approach the study of gender from different assumptions.

Structural-functionalists believe that men and women perform separate roles because this division is useful to society. For example, Talcott Parsons suggests the family is a social system with two major needs: getting its work done and staying in emotional order. Parsons believes men are 'naturally' more 'instrumental', or oriented toward getting work done, and women are 'naturally' more 'expressive', or oriented toward taking care of the family's socio-emotional needs. Functionalists see the division of labour in the family system according to gender as functional to the family and to society as a whole. Though such a division may have been useful to society in the past, sociologist began to question Parsons' conclusions as they grew more attuned to issues of inequality during the 1960s. In America, the Women's Movement sensitized people to the implications of neatly categorizing all economic behaviour as male and all nurturing behaviour as female. Today more adults have sought to form relationships in which both their instrumental and expressive traits can grow to their highest potential, whether they are men or women.

Conflict theory sees the almost universal inequality between the sexes in societies as an outgrowth of patriarchy, the form of social organization in which men dominate, or rule over, women (Collins, 1985). Patriarchy assumes that men are superior to women. This belief is based on sexism or the belief that one sex is inferior and thus deserves inferior treatment. Sexist beliefs continue to dominate our society and cause men to assume priviledge and women to assume secondary status. Just as racism caused blacks and other minority groups to doubt their self-worth, so sexism may affect a women's potential by limiting her own perceived horizons.

Friedrich Engels believed women in hunting and gathering societies were generally more socially equal to men than are women in industrialized societies. When horticulture was developed and land began to be owned and hence passed down from generation to generation, men became monogamous in order to assure that children who inherited their property were their own. This forced women into a subservient role, requiring them to be faithful to one husband and dependent upon his ability to fend for the family.

The main dimensions of sexual inequality are still seen in the varying degrees of access women and men have the power and wealth in society. Susan Chafetz writes about the many ways in which women are clearly still not as powerful as men in our society (Wallace & Wallace, 1989):

1. Women own fewer material goods and services.
2. They have less education.
3. They have less public and interpersonal decision-making power.
4. They hold fewer prestige-conferring roles, for instance, president of a group or organization.
5. They have fewer opportunities for enrichment and gratification.
6. They have fewer formal rights.
7. They own fewer life-sustaining necessities, for instance, property.

In addition, women must confront both societal constraints concerning proper behaviour for women and fear of physical coercion. For instance, only women need to fear for being raped on a date, or sexual harassment in the office. On all these dimensions, men and women clearly are not yet equal in our contemporary society.

This inherently unequal system affects the men in society as well. Many sociologists recognize that men are not free to develop the 'feminine' or nurturing aspects of their personalities as long as they are pressured to achieve and compete for resources. Men are subject to such constraints on their behaviour, for instance, as being thought less masculine if they express tender emotions.

IV

Anthropologists have looked for links between the development of sexual divisions of labour and the assignment of gender roles (Morris, 1978). His work suggests that sexual division of labour developed when people began to hunt for their food rather than simply to gather it. Men traveled after game, because the women were often nursing babies or taking care of young children. Evidence suggests, however, that at that time no status difference existed in their positions. Women were highly valued because they were the food gatherers. Desmond Morris (1978) explains this system and comments on its implications today:

> In our ancient past, women were absolutely at the centre of society. It was the hunters, the men, who went off to the periphery. There was a division of labour: females gathered and prepared food and reared the children. Males went off and hunted. But that division didn't mean that one sex was more important than the other. Women's liberation, I think, is becoming concerned with the wrong kinds of things. What really matters is that women should be given back their role of equal importance with men as members of society.

The change in status of women in cultures all over the world during the past decades clearly shows change in gender-role definition. It is possible that such roles have changed because women command more power in modern industrialized society than they did under former economic systems or because socialization practices have changed drastically. For instance, modern education and its subsequent (new) job opportunities alone have been re-shaping the role definition of Naga women over the years. If biology determined gender roles, every culture over time would make the same assumptions regarding the tasks of men and women. This did not happen. Instead, the world's cultures have a fascinating variety of ways to express gender.

Each Hopi Indian clan is headed by a woman and includes her brothers and sisters and all of their descendants. The mother's brother is the prime source of discipline for the children, who are given tasks according to their age and ability rather than their sex. The men and women work cooperatively in all areas, and treat each other equally. The Hopi never question the custom of a husband's living in the wife's home (Leavitt, 1970). But some of these customs would be quite unusual in a Naga society.

Margaret Mead's study of the three tribes in the South pacific is a landmark in cross-cultural gender-role research (Mead, 1935). Mead lived with the Arapesh, the Mundugumor, and the Tchambuli, carefully observing and minutely describing their customs and culture. She found all Arapesh people are expected to be loving, considerate, and cooperative. Both men and women tend children and are responsible for food. The Mundugumor, in sharp contrast, are usually aggressive, ruthless, and violent.

In the third tribe, the Tchambuli, the gender roles are differentiated as they are in western culture, but the Tchambuli women are the providers and dominate the men, having an impersonal attitude toward their families. Men, in contrast, are loving toward their children, less responsible for the economic needs of the family than are women, and more emotional.

Mead concluded from her studies that culture determines what is considered *'normal'* behaviour for a man or woman and that many of our *masculine'* or *'feminine'* traits are 'as lightly linked to sex as are the clothing, the manners, and the form of headdress that a society at a given period assigns to either sex'.

Richard Sorenson lived among the Fore in New Guinea

and observed changes in their gender roles that were obviously linked to changes in their social structures. The Fore had lived a communal life without chiefs or priests and shared all goods within the tribe.

The society of the Fore changed character drastically when a new road was built connecting their village with the outside world and the coffee plantations. Many of the men learned to cultivate coffee by working on the plantations and returned to the village to grow it there. Women continued their traditional tasks and took some of the men's former tasks. In contrast to their previous tranquility and harmony, the new Fore culture came to include 'many incidents of anger, withdrawal, aggressiveness, and stinginess'. The new society included more material wealth, at the cost of more competition, less relaxation, less involvement of father in the childrearing, more emphasis on exchange, and less on sharing. In short, their world had become more 'masculine' in modern Western terms, and given up its communal benevolent roots.

Other anthropologists since Mead and Sorenson also conclude that gender differences are primarily culturally determined and change as the culture changes.

One of the most interesting experiments in changing gender roles stereotypes was carried out in the kibbutz. A kibbutz is a collective farm or settlement in Israel. From its inception, the kibbutz was dedicated to the idea of equality of men and women. Women shared equally in the economic productivity of the kibbutz and were therefore not dependent on their husbands for the economic well-being. The community shared in raising the children, acquiring goods, and in household chores like cooking, laundry, and cleaning.

Gradually men and women reverted to more traditional male-female gender roles in the kibbutz. Mothers spent more time with the children, and the number of family activities increased. One researcher suggests that productive work in the kibbutz was always more prestigious than service work, and women were not allowed to do productive work as long as there was a pressing need for productive workers. Another researcher points out that although kibbutz men allowed women to take on traditional male productive roles, the men never developed a corresponding interest in traditionally female service roles. Rather, 'the emphasis was on changing women's roles without any corresponding change in men's roles'. This lack of commitment could be the variable which caused the reversal in female and male positions.

The People's Republic of China has experienced great change in attitudes toward gender roles, partly because its government has a high degree of control over its people. In the past, women were bought and sold, marriages were prearranged, rape was common, and women had 'no rights'.

Today, since China's Communist Revolution, the position of women in Chinese society has improved a great deal. The Marriage Law of 1950 gave women many new rights and abolished arranged marriages, the buying of wives, polygamy and child marriage. It provided procedures for divorce, for the re-marriage of widows, and for females to own property. Today more than 90 percent of Chinese women work outside their homes. They are represented in every occupation and receive equal pay for equal work. Their children are often cared for in well-run child-care centers near or in their places of work. The government has declared that men and women shall share household duties like cooking and cleaning (Tavris, 1974).

In spite of the gains for Chinese women, improvement is needed. As discussed earlier, new laws mandate only one child per family and strongly encourage abortion if a woman becomes pregnant a second time. Male children are still preferred by most mothers and fathers. Women are underrepresented at top levels of management, are more likely to be unemployed, and are less likely to be allowed to obtain well-paying heavy work.

In an Angami Naga society, though men and women work cooperatively and take responsibility for food, gender roles are clearly defined. For instance, in the jhum field, men slash and burn the vegetation to prepare the jhum sites; women clear the weeds, prepare the soil, transplant and cultivate. The society is highly characterized by many dos and don'ts for different gender. A woman in an Angami world is more burdened though men claim to do the harder works. There is a huge disparity between the tasks that women and men do in a day. In household chores, women not only have to nurture and raise children, but have to carry water, cook, and do laundry and cleaning. Both men and women are expected not only to know their roles but also to earnestly practice them. Women are expected to do multi-tasking. Even in urban settings, childcare is still the sole responsibility of a woman, despite the fact that women too earn an income outside their homes.

Very often, it is a problem of mindsets and attitudes. Patriarchy influences the worldview of women as much as it does that of men. Hence women themselves resist change unless they are trained to think out of the box of patriarchy (Mukhim, May 7, 2007). All this roles are defined and determined by their culture, customs, etc. It is the society which determines what role is normal for a man or what role is abnormal for a woman. However, no society can remain static as social change is universal; and with the changes in the social structures, the gender roles are changing.

A Case Example of an Angami Marriage

By examining this case example of an Angami Naga marriage, it gives a clear picture of changes on the one hand but continuity on the other. Though, the Angami group has embraced Christianity, the present marriage system is not totally Christian or totally traditional anymore. It is observed that though the proceedings and the forms of Christian marriage, marriageable age, selection of mate and the cost of marriage etc, have changed considerably, yet a Christian marriage still involves observance of the traditional customs such as the rule of exogamy, incest taboo, the community feast, exchange of gifts, the matrilineal inheritance and the bride-price although in a different form. Christianity has not taken away the traditional customs and culture from the Angami Nagas. No doubt, Christianity has initiated a process of far reaching social and cultural change among the group, but Naga Christianity is typically Naga in character. (Kikhi, 2008).

Marriage among the Angami Nagas is an important event

not only in the life of the persons who are getting married, but also for the households that are drawn together in matrimonial alliance. Marriage gives rise to affinal ties for wider networks of co-operation between individuals and households. The customary modes of incorporation and recruitment to the households among the Angamis are i) birth, ii) adoption and iii) marriage. A Christian marriage has not taken away these customary laws from the people. The basic and significant principle of membership into the household is therefore based on incorporation into the family. Birth is a principle by which an individual is incorporated into a family, while adoption is considered as a substitute to birth. On the other hand, marriage is a principle whereby a woman is recruited into her husband's household.

The Angami Nagas regard marriage as the normal state of life for every adult. There are very few persons who never marry. However, the number of unmarried persons seems to be increasing. Perhaps this has to do with modern education and related job facilities where woman are becoming more self-dependent. Again a qualified educated woman prefers to have an educated husband who is equally or more qualified. On the other hand, men prefers a wife who is less educated than him or equally educated but not more educated than him. Man seems to be apprehensive about marrying a more educated woman or equally educated woman, thinking she will dominate over him. Whatsoever, the Angamis attach immense importance to marriage, not only for the procreation of legitimate children, but also because no man or woman can adequately satisfy all his or her wants or lead a normal life, after reaching maturity, without a spouse (Das, 1993). Sooner or later a man must have a wife and a woman a husband. Among the Angami group traditionally 'land' and 'wives' have many common features. Land and wives stand for the fulfillment of fundamental social needs. However the importance of having land in the village seems to be loosing, as one would see many families moving out to cities and towns for jobs and education.

Marriage among the Angami Nagas is a systematically organized understanding between heads of two households whereby women are transferred and recruited into the households. Such a transaction follows reciprocal rights and obligations not only between two persons who are married but also between two households who form an affinal alliance. Therefore, at birth every Angami finds himself in a network of affinal relationships. An individual's own marriage establishes a new marriage transaction. Thus marriage among the Angamis establishes as well as transmits affinal ties between individuals and their households that are drawn into marriage alliance. In this fashion, each individual and his household find themselves in a network of affinal relationships in the kinship system of the society (Das, 1993).

The Angamis regard marriage as one of the important events in an individual's life. Parents take great responsibility to arrange the marriage of their children, which is considered as their foremost obligation. They consider leaving daughters unmarried blameworthy. It was a general practice to perform marriage of their daughters at an early age. However today, due to Christianity and formal education, girls are not married at an early age. In the past when a son or a daughter reaches adolescence, the parents look for the possible match and arrange the marriage. However, all marriages are not arranged. Even in the case of women she is given a freedom of choice. Her parents, it is true, may resort occasionally to a good deal of persuasion in regard to matrimonial projects. But they never resort to force, and cases of girls marrying against their inclination are exceedingly rare (Hutton, 1969).

Each marriage transaction takes place with reference to a body of rules with a distribution of values, which serve as general incentives and constraints on choices the Angamis make in the selection of spouses. These include the common rules of endogamy, incest and exogamy and certain other practical considerations, which their society demands.

V

Imagine how 'feminine' a girl would be if she was raised by her father and six brothers on a farm or ranch ninety miles from the nearest town. Assume, for good measure, she had no exposure to television, magazines, newspapers, or books. Or, think about how 'masculine a boy might be who is to be raised by his mother on the grounds of an isolated girls' academy. Now imagine a very different world totally void of social differences for the different genders. Families have identical expectations of sons and daughters. Children of both genders receive dolls, baseball gloves, training in how to play football or wrestling, and piano lessons. In all media, men and women act and dress in the same fashion. The language has been 'cleansed' of all gender cues. Half of all the secretaries are male and half of the executives or politicians are female. How much traditional 'feminine' and 'masculine' behaviour would survive in such an environment?

We would expect these unusual socialization environments to produce some unusual variations on the masculinity-femininity theme. The imaginary scenes suggest there are many modes through which a person is taught what is to be male or female in our culture (Wallace & Wallace, 1989).

Throughout our lives, we are presented with images of femininity and masculinity that help us accept these definitions while opposing any tendency to deviate from our culturally prescribed roles. The major agents of this socialization process are the family, the schools, the media, and the community.

A. Family Influences

Parents and family are, for most people, the dominant influence in shaping gender identity. From the moment of birth, gender is an important issue. 'It's a girl!' or 'It's a boy!' are likely to be the first words the physician speaks upon delivery of an infant. A mother dresses her infant in blue or pink so that even strangers can detect the gender and respond appropriately – and parents take offense at someone's mistaking their cute little girl for a handsome boy. Children are given a gender label from the start, and parents treat children according to the label (Wallace & Wallace, 1989).

As the child grows, gender identity is established through four processes:

1. Moulding, or reinforcement
2. Opportunities
3. Role modeling
4. Explicit verbal instruction.

One interesting experiment illustrates the *reinforcement* phenomenon. Researchers asked young mothers to play with a six-month-old infant dressed in a pink dress. Many said they could 'just tell' she was a girl, others stated that 'she cries more softly' than a boy. In the same study, other mothers were given a six-month-old in blue overalls. They smiled at this child less often, and offered him a doll to play with only one-third as often as they did to the pink-clothed child. The interesting twist in the experiment is that all the mothers played with the same child. Only the clothes and the name given to the baby were changed (Self & Datan, 1976). Obviously, these mothers treated the same infant differently only because of the infant's supposed gender.

Parents have been found to describe their newborn daughters as tiny, soft, fine-featured, and delicate, and to see their newborn sons as strong, alert, and well-coordinated. Parents will work harder to elicit smiling and cooing from daughters than from sons as early as age seven weeks (Moss, 1976). The teaching of desired feminine behaviour has begun, even though no difference in actual response between boys and girls is yet noticeable. One can also notice that as the time goes by, girls will be rewarded more for dependent behaviour. Boys may be given more freedom to be assertive. They are expected to break the bonds of dependence earlier than girls, and will be generally be cuddled for a shorter period of their lives than girls.

Families also provide different opportunities for boys and girls. Although girls may sometimes wear jeans, boys do not usually wear dresses or skirts. In this way, the masculine is more restricted than the feminine. On the other hand, girls are less likely than boys to receive toy guns, trucks, trains, or bats and balls, and boys are unlikely to receive dolls. Girls are more likely to be allowed access to their mother's old jewelry, dressy clothes, and high-heeled shoes. Boys are more likely to be taken along with Dad on 'masculine' trips such as fishing, or sports events like football, wrestling. In household chores, the parents differentiate strongly between boys and girls tasks. Thus boys are expected to chop firewood and help Dad in washing the car and girls assist Mom in the kitchen. Thus it is obvious that this system narrows the opportunities for children to widen their range of skills for adulthood.

Role modeling is a major mechanism of gender socialization. Even before they realize the sexual basis for gender labeling, children are well aware of masculine and feminine roles, and most children accept their categorization as a girl or a boy. A female child usually identifies with her mother and wants to be like her, and a male child usually wants to be like his father. As a result we can see that, girls are often interested in pretty clothes, hair-styles, makeup, and cooking. They develop the passive and gentle side of their personalities, if this is what they perceive in their role models. Boys become interested in tools, cars, and sports and they strive to be assertive and not to show their emotions. Role modeling is more effective when the child has a strong and warm relationship with the role model (Bandura, 1963).

Children learn through watching their parents and other adults interact, that gender is a basic principle in the organization of social life and that their world is patterned by it. They learn, for instance, that women avoid bad language and frequently phrase opinions in questions, whereas men state their opinion more directly and interrupt more frequently. Children see their fathers driving whenever both their parents are in the car and putting their arms around their mothers in a protective gesture. Children see man and older boys being rated on the basis of their aggressive abilities and women and older girls on the basis of their beauty. These implicit lessons are strong influences on the gender socialization process.

Some of the socialization into gender roles involves *explicit verbal instruction,* that is, the child is told that certain behaviour is or is not a part of the gender role: 'boys do not cry', 'girls are not supposed to let their slips or panties show', 'boys don't wear skirts', 'ladies before gentlemen', 'boys are stronger than girls'. Verbal instruction is probably less important than opportunity differences and role modeling.

B. Schools

In modern societies today, schools are important agents of gender socialization. The school continues the teaching of appropriate gender behaviour by teaching boys and girls appropriate behaviour in the wider outside world. This is also reflected in their behaviour, for example, girls most often do the 'housekeeping' and 'helping' chores of a classroom, while boys tend to be more defiant of their primarily female teachers, doing things like asking to go to the bathroom when they don't really need to. Boys typically play competitive, tough games in larger groups and monopolize the central play areas. Girls play more verbal and imaginative games in groups of two to four.

Within the classroom, students use text books to learn about the world outside their families and classrooms. Though text books do not directly address male and female role differences, they comment on gender roles through the actions of their characters and through the notable absence of female characters. Female and male characters provide models for young people who are forming self-identities. Raphaela Best calls these lessons in gender roles 'the second curriculum' (1983).

Various studies also reports that stories about girls are shorter and less interesting than those about boys. Males are generally presented in adventurous activities such as discovering oil or gold, playing ball, leading groups or resolving disputes. In contrast, the girls rarely left the confines of the family or received recognition of their achievements.

Fathers are portrayed as problem solvers, builders, controllers, and creators, whereas a mother is shown as 'a pleasant, hardworking, emotional, and caring.

Children's leisure reading also influences their gender role assumptions. Children's literature contains stereotypic behaviour that describes traditional male and female gender roles. The first major study done in this area found that prizewinning children's books contained eleven pictures of males to every one picture of a female, and one-third of the books had no female characters at all (Weitzman & Eifler, 1972). Women in the stories were all housewives, and none of the fathers helped in work around the house. In reality, 42 percent of women with children fewer than 6 years of age and 58 percent of women with children 6 to 17 years of age were working outside the home the year the books were studied.

Romance novels, now popular among young teenage girls, depict women as victims of male aggression and define women only in relationship to their aggressors. In ways children's literature give a distorted picture of actual behaviour in the society.

Schools also channel students toward gender roles in other ways. Many courses are distinctly gender-segregated. Physical education classes have traditionally been segregated by gender, although this is changing in many parts of the world. Certain classes, such as sewing or home science, are seldom chosen by males, and others such as NCC are rarely chosen by females. Again boys far outnumber girls in high school and college computer courses, although computer knowledge will be essential for tomorrow's leaders. Furthermore, in all classes, teachers praise boys more than girls, give boys more academic help, and are more likely to accept boys' comments in classroom discussions.

In extra-curricular activities, cheerleaders are usually girls, whereas the major school sports figures are usually boys. Many sports played against other schools are restricted to one sex, as wrestling, football, field hockey, and volleyball.

C. Media & Advertising

In addition to the influence of family and schools, most people are exposed to massive doses of television, popular music, motion pictures, magazines, and newspapers. Perhaps media has become the most influential agent of socialization in the modern context. Although some media address factual matters, most material presented is selected for entertainment. What is transmitted, therefore, is not a realistic portrayal but an exaggerated version of social life. Gender images are often caricatures of either the audience's or the sponsor's ideal people. Thus, an audience ideal male is not just brave; he is ridiculously brave, incredibly good-looking, crafty, and lucky. The female ideal is a superwoman who is beautiful, cunning, tolerant, and properly fulfills the male's adolescent sex fantasies (Wallace & Wallace, 1989).

The images of men and women that television and magazine advertisers promote are usually flattering to the intended consumer. Sponsors may also portray the genders in ways that are appealing to the opposite sex, for example, a 'classy young woman' approving the product. In today's advertising, women are most often portrayed in the home instead of in an outside occupation, and men's voices are almost exclusively used as the background 'voice of authority'. Male actors or sportsman are chosen to sell financial services and expensive household purchases such as cars, whereas women are most often in ads for food, clothes, and household cleaners.

The media do not transmit a unified image of male and female gender roles, but portray traditional roles, caricatured ideal roles, and occasionally egalitarian roles. People in our society today spend a great deal of time with the media and the media strongly influence their perceptions of gender roles.

D. Culture

The culture environment influences definitions of appropriate gender role behaviour. The socially shared ideas of how women and men should act are transmitted in diverse ways, including differences in language and observed interactions with the institutions of society.

The language offers no easy way to discuss a person without revealing his or her gender. From birth, children are given names that serve as gender labels. Every time someone refers to someone else, it is either by using the person's name or by a personal pronoun (he or she) that states gender. For instance in a Naga society usually the names clearly spells out to which gender one belongs. Or the personal pronoun of all age group clearly differentiates the gender. In virtually every discussion of a person, gender is revealed, but not necessarily age, race, ethnic background, religion, or social status. This constant reminder of who is male and who is female contributes to gender socialization, because it helps us to make associations between gender and behaviour.

Another aspect of language that help people learn their gender identity is the presence of gender-linked derogatory names, like calling a male a 'sissy' or a female an 'old maid'. This not only describes but also condemns the person. Such name-calling teaches people what males and females should *not* be and provides strong social control over gender roles. It is interesting to note that corresponding terms are much less derogatory for males. For instance, 'bachelor', the logical correlate of 'old maid' does not carry the strong condemnation of the term used for women.

We learned much of our gender-role expectations by observing and participating in male and female behaviour in society's institutions. Today's women play minor roles in the major institutions of government, religion, economics, and education. Although, in many states, women voters equals if not outnumber men, female members in religious organizations and schools is similar in proportion to that of men, and the number of women in government offices is approaching to that of men, few women hold leadership positions in government, religion, education, or industry. For that matter, one can question why there are no women priests among Roman Catholics, or women pastors among the Baptists or Presbyterians? In terms of occupying powerful and prestigious positions in these institutions, women are still a minority. Male and female children observe this and assume these future roles for themselves.

In the family, women are still socially central and dominant, organizing and leading most family activities. Women usually tend the children, cook, clean or supervise cleaning, women do the shopping and they arrange the social calendar. Women claim the house or major portions of it as their 'turf'. Thus, a wife may even refer to the kitchen as 'my kitchen' or to the living room as 'my living room', and she would not like her children or husband to 'invade' this territory with their activities.

In order to come to parity with men in other institutions, women must achieve cooperation within the family. Perhaps we should move to a system in which men and women 'share the chores of home and children according to their abilities and needs'. The house would be a shared territory both in terms of use and responsibility like in China.

Boys would have to be socialized to assume equal responsibility in the traditionally female-dominated family and girls would have to grow to expect cooperation among all the family members in household tasks. Until this occurs, women who choose to enter the paid work force, which is currently male dominated, usually are required to fill two full-time positions: one at work and one at home resulting into role-conflict.

Thus, many different agents socialize us into gender roles. Families give the earliest reinforcement for acting appropriately according to one's gender, and society continues to teach what is acceptable and what is not for men and for women. Gender roles are demonstrated and reinforced in almost every aspect of one's social life.

VI

The umbrella term status of women obscures many variations depending on the dimension of stratification (power, prestige, property) and the institutional sphere (family, economy, politics, education, religion). Great differences also exist within the population of women - by age, race, ethnic origin, and social class. The status of women is highly variable across cultures and within any society.

Since the early 1960s, the women's movement has spread across the globe. The strength and structure of women's organizations will vary from one society to another, as will their immediate goals and tactics. The basic goals essential to gender equality everywhere are the right to vote, to control fertility, to receive an education, and to keep one's own earnings or inherited property. In these terms, the countries of Northern

Europe, come closest to an egalitarian ideal, followed by Canada, Israel, and the United States, with much of Africa and the Muslim world least egalitarian. But even in many traditional societies, the ideas and ideals of the women's movement have led some women to protest openly, at great personal risk (Afary, 1994). At the very least, once-tolerated practices of female subordination have been challenged and exposed to international view. It is probably safe to say that gendered stratification systems will never be quite the same.

The goal of the New Feminist Movement is to challenge gendered inequality in major institutional spheres: the family, economy, politics, health care system, religion, education, and law. All these movements were successful in one way or the other and have set new trends for women and have brought about political, educational, business, occupational and financial gains.

Various women movements directly or indirectly have initiated changes in educational opportunities. Female enrollment in schools and colleges has drastically risen. The percentage of women graduates and female PhD recipients are increasing. In a state like Nagaland, recent trend shows that girls are performing better than boys in exams like NPSC, HSLC and others. The percentage of women in fields like engineering and medical are also increasing. Women are choosing prestigious and lucrative fields of study rather than traditionally female areas like teaching and nursing.

Partly due to changes in women's educational levels and partly even due to the pressure to admit women to new fields, women's occupational status is changing gradually. Today a large percentage of the women in work force group are employed outside the home. A sizeable percentage of women are available in blue-collar jobs previously closed to them in many societies. The number of female professionals is increasing as lawyers, medical doctors, or even women executives.

Although the numbers of women in these positions have increased positively, men still tend to dominate many high status positions in society. For instance, women are much underrepresented at universities, although more women are teaching in colleges and schools. Similarly, although many women are now executives, comparatively few of them are in the very top management group. Women are also underrepresented as secretaries and heads of various departments.

Women's earnings, however have not kept place as compared to men. In the past, industry has claimed that the discrepancy in earnings is accounted for by the fact that women have less education, often take time off from careers to raise children, and work in less lucrative areas than men. There is also discrepancy in the availability of jobs for men and women. Women workers enter a labour force that is thoroughly gendered. Most employed women today work at dead-end jobs in the service sector. Then, what is a fair wage? Or as such, the question of gender wage gap arises. The gender wage gap refers to the discrepancy between average earnings of women and men.

In today's world the working mother has to balance office work and household work, often resulting in role conflict if not handled properly. On this line, Lisa Belkin says, mothers should warn their children (daughters) about the bad times they may have to face; mothers should teach the children the fine art of balancing work and parenting (*The Telegraph*, May 15, 1997). Research findings indicates that if women and men share domestic tasks equally, their pay, occupational distributions, and rates of work-force participation would be more equal. Currently, however, few men even come close to sharing housework equally with their wives. One reason men hesitate to do traditional female tasks is that those tasks are often seen as less valuable to society than traditional male tasks.

Gains for women have been made in other areas also. More women are entering government jobs from the local to the national level. However women still have lower percentage of members in parliaments, assemblies, autonomous councils, municipalities, or even local bodies like panchayats. For instance, 33 percent reservation for women in parliament is a far cry still. The same parliament which set up the Parliamentary Committee, recommending 33 percent reservation of seats for women, could not even come to a consensus to pass the reservation bill.

The female candidate is no longer an oddity as both male and female voters at all social class levels have become more accepting. However, women candidates have more difficulty in raising money and in being perceived as a forceful leader as compared to her male counterpart. People still tend to remember what a male candidate said and what a female candidate wore. Opportunities are even more limited for women of colour, who are greatly underrepresented in elective offices compared with their male counterparts (Hess, Markson & Stein, 2000).

Throughout the industrialized world and in developing nations women are slowly moving into national politics. Women actually won the right to vote in national elections in France in1944 and Switzerland in 1971. Where women have been elected or appointed to office, they typically occupy positions associated with women's interest such as health, education and welfare rather than defense and finances. Nonetheless, since the 1990's more than a dozen nations all over the world has either had a woman as a Prime Minister or President, which definitely speaks volumes that women can equally compete with men in areas of administration and leadership. Again, in the 1990s Norwegian prime minister Gro Harlem Brundtland had almost 40 percent women cabinet. The experience suggests that as more women are elected to political office, greater attention will be paid to 'women issues' such as child-care subsidies, paid parental leave, and other benefits for working parents and children.

Overall, although the presence of women in positions of political and economic power is only slightly greater than it was a few decades ago. A determined and talented few who are also wives and mothers will make it to the highest levels with the assistance of a supportive husband, affordable child care, and household help. Most, however, will face the choice between fulfilling career dreams and the demands of parenthood.

To conclude, sociologists generally agree that women and men fit their gender roles largely because they are socialized to do so. Gender differences are primarily culturally determined and will effectively change as culture changes.

The changes that have evolved in the definitions of gender roles will undoubtedly suggest changes in social institutions as well. Marriages and families will continue to make many adjustments to the new roles of women. Government and economic positions will continue to open to women, and the institutions have to adapt to a new style of working as more and more women enter them. Education is one key agent to train women (men and children as well) to receive advanced degrees in order to fit into different level jobs.

It is a problem of mindsets and attitudes. Patriarchy influences the worldview of women as much as it does that of men. Hence women themselves resist change unless they are trained to think out of the box of patriarchy. India, as a country, is steeped in patriarchal values, and gender seems to be only a politically correct stance we take at meetings and discussions. Policies have to be planned with a gender perspective to expect gender outcomes at the implementation stage. This will enable them to participate in decision-making about their own income, welfare, reproductive rights.

Although this country has attempted to bring gender as a cross-cutting theme in policy-making, the results are not visible as yet. Gender disparities abound. We have 'come a long way', but we have only made progress toward changing the situation rather than eradicating it.

REFERENCES

1. Afary, Janet; 1994; 'From Radical Democracy to Militant Islam: The Iranian Women's Movement in the 20th Century', Paper presented at the *XII World Congress of Sociology*; Bielefeld, Germany; July.

2. Anandhi, S & Padmini Swaminathan; 2006; 'Making It Relevant: Mapping the Meaning of Women's Studies in Tamil Nadu', *Economic and Political Weekly;* Oct 21-27, Vol XLI, No. 42, pp 4444-4454.

3. Bandura, Albert & Richard H. Walters; 1963; *Social Learning and Personality Development;* New York; Rinehart & Winston.

4. Belkin, Lisa; 2007; 'Climb Every Mountain', *The Telegraph*; Tuesday, May 15, 2007.

5. Bem, Sandra Lipsitz; 1993; *The Lenses of Gender: Transforming the Debate on Sexual Inequality;* New Haven; CT: Yale University Press.

6. Best, Raphaela; 1983; *We've All Got Stars: What Boys and Girls Learn in Elementary School;* Bloomington; University of Indiana Press.

7. Bottomore, T.B; 1986; *Sociology: A Guide to Problems and Literature* (Revised Edition). New Delhi; Blackie & Son (India) Ltd.

8. Christina, Kekhrieseno; 2002; 'Customary Laws and the Women's Development in Nagaland' in C. Joshua Thomas and Gurudas Das (ed.), *Dimensions of Development in Nagaland;* New Delhi; Regency Publications.

9. Collins, Randall; 1985; *Sociology of Marriage and the Family;* Chicago; Nelson Hall.

10. Devika, J & Mini Sukumar; 2006; 'Making Space for Feminist Social Critique in Contemporary Kerala', *Economic and Political Weekly;* Oct 21-27, Vol XLI, No. 42, pp 4469-4475.

11. Eitzen, D. Stanley and Maxine Baca-Zinn; 1994; *Social Problems;* (6th Edition) Boston; Allyn and Bacon.

12. Gilmore, David G; 1990; *Manhood in the Making: Cultural Concepts of Masculinity;* New Haven; CT: Yale University Press.

13. Haralambos, M & R.M. Heald; 2006; *Sociology: Themes and Perspectives;* New York; Oxford University Press.

14. Harrington, Michael; 1984; *The New American Poverty*; New York; Holt, Rinehart, and Winston.

15. Hess, Beth B, Elizabeth W. Markson & Peter J. Stein; 2000; *Sociology* (Fifth Edition); London; Allyn and Boston.

16. Kikhi, Kedilezo; 2008; 'Changes and Continuity in Naga Marriage: Case Study of Zounuo-Keyhonuo Group of Angami-Naga', in T.B. Subha, J. Puthenpurakal & Shaji Joseph Puykunnel (ed.), *Christianity and Change in Northeast India;* New Delhi; Concept Publishing Company.

17. Kishor, Sunita; 1993; 'May God Give Sons to All: Gender and Child Mortality in India', *American Sociological Review*; 58, pp 247-256.

18. Krishnaraj, Maithreyi; 2006; 'Is "Gender" Easy to Study? Some Reflections', *Economic and Political Weekly;* Oct 21-27, Vol XLI, No. 42, pp 4440-4443.

19. Leavitt, Ruby R; 1970; 'Women in Other Cultures' in *Sex Roles in Changing Society;* New York; Random House.

20. Long, Russ; 2005; *Institutional Discrimination: Gender Stratification.*

21. Mead, Margaret; 1935; *Sex and Temperament in Three Primitive Societies;* New York; Morrow.

22. Moore, Wilbert E; 1994; *Social Change (Second Edition)*; New Delhi; Prentice Hall of India Pvt. Ltd.

23. Morris, Desmond; 1978; 'Understanding the Beast in All of Us: An Interview with Desmond Morris by Gerald Clarke', *Family Circle;* (May 19), pp 68-77.

24. Moss, Howard; 1976; 'Are We Born into Our sex Roles or Programmed into Them', *Woman's Day;* January.

25. Mukhim, Patricia; 2007; 'Gender & Development', *The Telegraph;* May 7, 2007.

26. Munshi, Indra; 2006; 'Tourism Processes and Gender Relations: Issues for Exploration and Intervention', *Economic and Political Weekly;* Oct 21-27, Vol XLI, No. 42, pp 4461-4468.

27. Reinharz, Shulamit; 1986; "Patriarchal Pontifications", *Society;* Vol 23, pp 23-28.

28. Self, Patricia & Nacy Datan; 1976; 'Are We Born into Our sex Roles or Programmed into Them', *Woman's Day;* January.

29. Sen, Amartya; 1990; 'More Than 100 Million Women Are Missing', *New York Review of Books;* December 20, pp 61-66.

30. Sorenson, E. Richard; 1971; *The Evolving Force: A Study of Socialization and Cultural Change in the New Guinea Highlands;* Palo Alto; CA: Stanford University Press.

31. Tavris, Carol; 1974; 'Field Report: Women in China, the Speak-Bitterness Revolution', *Psychology Today;* pp 43-98.

32. Thakur, Ravni; 2006; 'Women's Studies in China Today' in *Economic and Political Weekly;* Oct 21-27, Vol XLI, No. 42, pp 4455-4460.

33. Tumin, Melvin M; 1994; *Social Stratification: the forms and functions of inequality* (Second Edition); New Delhi; Prentice Hall of India Pvt. Ltd.

34. United Nations; 1993; *Report on the World Situation;* New York; United Nations Publications.

35. Wallace, Richard Cheever & Wendy Drew Wallace; 1989; *Sociology* (2nd Edition); London; Allyn and Bacon.

36. Weitzman, Lenore J & Deborah Eifler; 1972; 'Sex Role Socialization in Picture Books for Pre-school children', *American Journal of Sociology;* 77, pp 1125-1144.

37. 'China Warns of Population Rebound', *The Times of India;* Tuesday, May 8, 2007.

38. 'Married to Materialism', *The Times of India;* Tuesday, May 8, 2007.

2

Globalization and Empowerment of Women: An Observation in Indian Context

Arjun Das

[Globalization has brought tremendous opportunities as well as disadvantages for the cross-sections of people on different angle. It has opened up new challenges towards civilization. Therefore, social scientists around the world are busy in analyzing the factors affecting the society as a whole for the formation of a healthy civil society. Under this backdrop this article is an attempt to observe the issues concerning women empowerment in the context of globalization.]

What Globalization is?

First of all it is better to clarify that the term "globalization" is very difficult to define in literary terms so far it is used in so many ways and in such varied contexts that it seems almost futile to attempt a universally acceptable definition for it. It is so because various scholars and social scientists have discussed the impact of globalization on every aspect of human existence, namely, politics, economics, religion, culture, knowledge, science and so on. As a matter of fact globalization is seen as a world-wide phenomenon or process. In the economic context the term globalization is a combination of some economic or monetary policies which, when adopted, may lead to the process of globalization. In the economic context the process of globalization has many dimensions. The first among these is the expansion of international trade. Second is the migration of people to various parts of the world. Third is the flow of cash and other investments amongst nations. The fourth dimension is the capital investment by firms or citizens of one nation to another for purposes of producing industrial, agricultural and consumer goods and then marketing them. Another aspect of globalization is the exchange of finance capital between nations or regions. The sixth aspect concerns the impact and influence of multinational companies or transnational corporations (MNCs/TNCs) on trade, investment and production. Next is the exchange of technology between countries and finally the expansion of international communication networks and the impact of electronic technology on the media in different lands.

The term "globalization" describes the increased mobility of goods, services, labour, technology and capital throughout the world. Although globalization is not a new development, its pace has increased with the advent of new technologies, especially in the area of telecommunications. It is to be mentioned here that many strands of globalization has its roots many centuries before the origin of modern capitalism. It is so because the history of transcontinental and transnational migration is ancient. Similarly the spread of technology is also a matter of ancient history. When the ancestors of modern man progressed from the hunting-gathering-survival stage to the taming of animals and cultivation of food, these technologies spread to almost every human group more than five to six thousand years ago. This was followed by the globalization of the use of copper, bronze, iron and other metal alloys. With the beginning of commerce came the exchange of goods and technologies between different civilizations. Evidence has been found of trade and commerce and technological exchanges between Harappa and Mohenjodaro and Assyrian civilizations, as between the Gangetic and Roman and Greek civilizations. There is evidence of international flow of traders and settlers all over the world. Since the 8th century A.D. and even earlier, Indian traders had formed their settlements in different regions of South-east Asia and a little later in East Africa and its adjoining areas.

Broadly speaking experts believe that this system evolved between the 15th and 16th centuries A.D. In the Western and Southern European nations, the combined effect of the rise of naval powers, support of the rulers and the enterprise of sailors and traders was such that it opened the routes of transatlantic passage to the two vast continents of North and South America and set in motion the exploitation at will of the human and natural resources available there. Almost simultaneously these western and southern European nations also 'discovered' the sea route to India and south-east Asia sailing from Europe around the southern tip and eastern coast of Africa. As a result of the opening up of these intercontinental sea routes, the control of European traders and ruling classes on overseas trade gradually increased as did the pace and flow of trade. With the total backing and support of their respective governments in 17th century A.D. emerged the East India Companies of England and Holland and a few others like the Ostend and Royal Africa Companies which may be considered the predecessors of the present day multinational companies. The East India Company of England and the East India Company of Netherlands in time established the British and Dutch rule in India and Indonesia respectively. With the spread of capitalism, finance capital kept flowing outward from nations. First Amsterdam, then London and Paris and finally New York and Tokyo and Frankfurt became the centres of the Capital market. Prior to the 19th century A.C., foreign investments were restricted to cash crops like sugarcane, cotton and indigo and the manufacture of sugar from cane. From the 19th century onwards we see the beginnings of direct foreign investments in every country in many other areas like the manufacturing of handlooms, electrical and other appliances and machines, mineral oil and other mineral products and the production of consumer goods. It was at this point that a new kind of multinational company was born.

Similarly at the end of the 19th century in many countries, specially non-white foreign ruled ones and in Latin America unrestricted trade policies gained ground with the total support of the British government. Thenceforth the flow of international trade changed its shape from that of a stream to a vast ocean.

Between the 17th and 19th centuries A.C., the trade of another cruel commodity took on an enormous dimension and it was North America and Europe that became the users of this novel merchandise. This inhuman commodity was a huge mass of captive slaves brought from Africa. Every year thousands of men, women, children and youth were enchained and shipped across the Atlantic to the Caribbean islands, to Brazil, Mexico and the United States of America and deployed there as slaves. Many among them embraced death while at sea. About one crore and twenty lakh slaves were transported from Africa in this manner. This horrible aspect of globalization almost devastated the whole of western, southern and eastern Africa. Starting from the 19th century and continuing up to the second decade of the 20th century another stream of humanity spread all over the world. This stream comprised the ordinary European migrants and numbered more than 4 crores of people. These whites established their colonies in the Americas, New Zealand, South Africa and Australia by first eliminating or repressing the native inhabitants of these regions. Around the same time a few lakh people from India also migrated to Mauritius, Fiji, Trinidad, Barbados, Natal and other regions as bonded labour. In Europe after the Second World War, migrant workers from Turkey, Greece, Algeria and Morocco were employed in post-war reconstruction work in Germany and France, just as lakhs migrated from the Caribbean isles and the Indian subcontinent to lives of hard labour and low wages in factories, buses, trains and ships of Britain. There was also the incidence of lakhs of people migrating legally and illegally into the USA from Mexico and Latin America to seek livelihood and sustenance. The World Bank, the International Monetary Fund, the United States, Britain, Germany, France and other wealthy nations are great advocates of globalization in all matters. The process of globalization gained momentum in different periods during the rapid advance of the capitalist system. From the second half of the 19th century trade and investments in white-ruled colonies and the migration of Europeans to other countries with the aim of establishing colonies, happened at a very fast pace. However, all of this movement stagnated during the period between the two World

Wars, which was the longest critical spell faced by the capitalist system. Again in the post-second World War era, particularly in the three decades of fierce competition between the USA and USSR for the position of world superpower, direct and indirect capital investment, world-wide trade flows and the spread of multinational companies gained great speed.

In this way if we trace back the root to the concept of globalization it will be a long history. So in short the term "Globalization" is the inexorable integration of markets, nation-states, and technologies to a degree never witnessed before—in a way that is enabling individuals, corporations, and nation-states to reach around the world farther, faster, deeper, and cheaper that ever before, and in a way that is enabling the world to reach into individuals, corporations, and nation-states farther, faster, deeper than ever before." (Friedman, p. 9)

"The driving idea behind globalization is free-market capitalism – the more you let market forces rule and the more you open your economy to free trade and competition, the more efficient and flourishing your economy will be. Globalization means the spread of free-market capitalism to virtually every country in the world. Globalization also has its own set of economic rules – rules that revolve around opening, deregulating and privatizing your economy." (Friedman, p. 9).

Globalization - Some Definitions

Jan Aart Scholte (2000: 15-17) has argued that at least five broad definitions of 'globalization' can be found in the literature.

Globalization as internationalization - Here globalization is viewed 'as simply another adjective to describe cross-border relations between countries'. It describes the growth in international exchange and interdependence. With growing flows of trade and capital investment there is the possibility of moving beyond an inter-national economy, (where 'the principle entities are national economies') to a 'stronger' version - the globalized economy in which, 'distinct national economies are subsumed and rearticulated into the system by international processes and transactions' (Hirst and Peters 1996: 8 and 10).

Globalization as liberalization - In this broad set of definitions, 'globalization' refers to 'a process of removing government-imposed restrictions on movements between countries in order to create an "open", "borderless" world economy' (Scholte 2000: 16). Those who have argued with some success for the abolition of regulatory trade barriers and capital controls have sometimes clothed this in the mantle of 'globalization'.

Globalization as universalization - In this use, 'global' is used in the sense of being 'worldwide' and 'globalization' is "the process of spreading various objects and experiences to people all over the world". A classic example of this would be the spread of computing, television etc.

Globalization as westernization or modernization - (especially in an 'Americanized' form). Here 'globalization' is understood as a dynamic, 'whereby the social structures of modernity (capitalism, rationalism, industrialism, bureaucratism, etc.) are spread the world over, normally destroying pre-existent cultures and local self-determination in the process.

Globalization as deterritorialization - (or as the spread of supraterritoriality). Here 'globalization' entails a 'reconfiguration of geography, so that social space is no longer wholly mapped in terms of territorial places, territorial distances and territorial borders. Anthony Giddens' has thus defined globalization as ' the intensification of worldwide social relations which link distant localities in such a way that local happenings are shaped by events occurring many miles away and vice versa. (Giddens 1990: 64). David Held et al. (1999: 16) define globalization as a ' process (or set of processes) which embodies a transformation in the spatial organization of social relations and transactions – assessed in terms of their extensity, intensity, velocity and impact- generating transcontinental or inter-regional flows and networks of activity'.

Indian Society and Globalization

As per the process of structural adjustment due to globalization the Indian Society is rapidly changing. According to Desrechers "Cultural imperialism has two major goals-one economic and the other political merely to take control of the markets for its cultural commodities and to establish hegemony by shaping popular consciousness...Cultural domination is an integral dimension of any sustained system of global exploitation." Due to the impact of globalization the traditional values of family system in Indian scenario have seen changing and thereby the nuclear family system is gaining momentum and has become the norm resulting in marriages breaking up. The reason behind is modern life style, professional ambitions in the corporate world for capital gain. The consumerism culture has ignited to change the very fabric of traditional Indian society. Since our attention in this article is to observe on globalization and empowerment of women it is better to analyze those factors which are affecting the women folk towards empowering them for their overall development. As we see for majority of women globalization has attributed to displacement, commodification and modern day slavery of women in Asian countries. As a result of that thousands of women are going to other countries to find better opportunities. Migration policies by sending governments have encouraged the trafficking in women, as trading is clearly seen in the commodification of women's bodies through prostitution. Abuse of women was prevalent in India before globalization but during globalization the trend has increased because of the stress and strain of the community and the changes in the traditional life style. Indian women have been suffering under many traditional evils, such as dowry and inequality even before major globalization.

It is a fact that the process of globalization has increased the greed of people for more goods and as a result more dowry is demanded from women. This has made it worse for young women and their parents to meet the dowry demands of a new TV, car and such other luxurious articles. Studies and research shows that educated women compared to the uneducated lot get and enjoy elementary human rights and other benefits. Thus women's education has set an example on social development (Usha Narayanan, 1994, p.7).

Indian Women's Status in the Changing World

Research and all kinds of activism have presently focused on the negative fallout of the process of globalization and liberalization on women. They have stressed the need that the investment in the social sector be increased. But a government on opening up the economy to foreign investment and free trade has paid no heed to these voices, although India has experienced industrial recession and a period of jobless growth in the past decade. Given the high levels of the population and a large population below age 20, the demand for employment is growing and joblessness and accompanying frustrations have contributed to violence, frequently expressed as ethnic, caste, class or communal conflicts. Women are the worst sufferers in such conflicts. The government has declared 2001 as the Year of Women's Empowerment or Swashakti. A policy for the Empowerment of Women was drafted in 1996 but has been in cold storage since then. It was passed in March 2001 by the Cabinet but miles to go practically. Despite all the official proclamations about empowerment and the numerous government schemes designed to improve women's economic conditions, their material status still shows much cause for concern.

Globalization has presented new challenges for the realization of the goal of women's equality, the gender impact of which has not been systematically evaluated fully. However, from the micro-level studies that were commissioned by the Department of Women & Child Development, it is evident that there is a need for re-framing policies for access to employment and quality of employment. Benefits of the growing global economy have been unevenly distributed leading to wider economic disparities, feminization of poverty, increased gender inequality through deteriorating working conditions and unsafe working environment especially in the informal economy and rural areas. Strategies will have to be designed to enhance the capacity of women and empower them to meet the negative social and economic impacts, which may flow from the globalization process.

In short the National Policy *for the empowerment of women (2001)* says that the principle of gender equality is enshrined in the Indian Constitution in its Preamble, Fundamental Rights, Fundamental Duties and Directive Principles. The Constitution not only grants equality to women, but also empowers the State to adopt measures of positive discrimination in favour of women.

Within the framework of a democratic polity, our laws, development policies, plans and programmes have aimed at women's advancement in different spheres. From the Fifth Five Year Plan (1974-78) onwards has been a marked shift in the approach to women's issues from welfare to development. In recent years, the empowerment of women has been recognized as the central issue in determining the status of women. The National Commission for Women was set up by an Act of Parliament in 1990 to safeguard the rights and legal entitlements of women. The 73rd and 74th Amendments (1993) to the Constitution of India have provided for reservation of seats in the local bodies of Panchayats and Municipalities for women, laying a strong foundation for their participation in decision making at the local levels.

In the light of the National Policy as well as other policies as declared from time to time by the government let us see the real plight of the women at different sectors:

Health

National policy envisages equal access to women to health care: The National Health Policy 2001 promises increased access to women for basic health care and commits highest priority to funding identified programmes relating to women's health. But poverty, early marriage, malnutrition and lack of health care during pregnancy are the major reasons for mortality rate for infant as well as for the mother. Maternal mortality in India is the second highest in the world. In this regard poverty and lack of awareness also hinder mothers from giving adequate care for their children. Social restrictions on women's mobility also contribute to lesser healthcare for women and children.

Education

Census carried out in 1951 recorded that only 25 percent

of men and 7 percent of women were literate. If we see the present trend in terms of literacy and education, India still contains the largest number of illiterate people in the world and also the largest number of illiterate women. It is so because the progress of improvement in literacy has been very slow and the literacy among females remains substantially below males and that even at present, nearly half the female population of the country remains illiterate. Moreover, female literacy rates are much lower especially among SC and ST castes as well as among certain minority groups. Keeping in view of the fact women's movement has repeatedly called upon the government to fulfill its pledge to increase investment in GDP towards education sectors.

Employment

It is observed that liberalization has caused an increasing inequality in employment opportunities and incomes and the economic opportunities created by liberalization are highly unequal. It is so because those better accesses with modern professional courses and skills suited for MNC's and other corporate world with modern link internationally have been able to get the benefit. Globalization has created nothing but new opportunity for women at the upper-income level having upper-skill. To aggravate the situation liberalization has in some sectors caused loss of employment without creation of new employment. Unemployment and underemployment rates are higher among women than among men. The same is true of educated women. Among tertiary education graduates "the rate of unemployment was less than 9% for men but 27% for women". Lower literacy rates have resulted in fewer women in employment categories which require higher educational and professional training. Overall, female participation rate in the labour force is 32% with variations between states. The states of Tamil Nadu, Kerala, Andhra Pradesh and Maharashtra show much "higher rates of work participation than the major northern and eastern states". Nationally, women only make up 18% of the formal sector and only 9.2% of employed women hold full-time positions, compared to 18% of employed men.

Women's Social Status and Social Security

Social status for women during the on going process of globalization has made her life from bad to worse at different social angles. The burning problem is that the crime rate against women has been rising with each year. Even law makers are under scanner for inflicting suffering against women. MP's are also found associated with woman trafficking. Social security still eludes for women workers. In the unorganized sector or informal economy social security is a far cry for women and the problem is very much acute for women as they play the triple role of a worker, housewife and mother. The lack of capital and assets, low and irregular income, aided by frequent accidents, sickness and such other factors drag these women into deprivation to live a decent life. In absence of any comprehensive and user friendly mechanism for proper implementation of various schemes meant for social security which has to benefit women they are suffering a lot at different steps.

Political Participation and Legal Position for Women

During freedom struggle Indian women played equal role like men but the hard reality is that it did not translate into continued participation for women in public life. Women's representation in state assembly and in Lok Sabha remains low. Hence women's movement at various capacities is pressing hard for the reservation of one-third of seats in the Lok Sabha. Indian constitution lays down equal status for women but many anomalies remain under different laws which, needs urgent amendment keeping in mind the greater interest for women as well as for the nation.

In these ways we have seen that there remains lot of other sectors which need urgent attention in areas such as Economic Participation, Access to Technology, Poverty alleviation, Human Rights, Training , Participation in Decision Making, Violation Against Women, Role of Media etc. for the sole benefit of women in the changing world.

Globalization of Media and its Impact on Women towards Empowerment

Considering the impact of media both Electronic as well as Print Media can be effectively used as a powerful tool for social change. The government has adopted two approaches to use it as an instrument of change and to control its possible misuse. An integrated media campaign to project a positive image of women and the girl child is an important component of Government's communication strategy. There is an increased presence of women in managing media and in gender sensitization of the media in depiction of sensitive issues. Media is encouraged to develop a code of conduct, professional guidelines, other self-regulatory mechanisms to remove gender stereotypes, and promote balanced portrayals of women and men. But the policy so far adopted by the Indian Government is not sufficient enough to control the situation adequately since an unequal flow of information regarding gender biases in media policy still continue to play an important role in depicting violence against women, pornography and also implications of satellite and telecommunications technology including issues of Internet usage and pornography on the net. The issues have added more complex layers to women, media relationship.

The complex dimension is added to the analysis in realizing the impact of the media on women's lives as viewed by feminists on the issue of pornography and its regulation. Some feminists opine that the call for more stringent regulation could become a threat to freedom of expression; others perceive pornography as a form of violence against women that cannot go unchecked. So the dilemma for many feminists becomes complex. Similarly the question of the media's treatment of violence against women also sees competing discourse .As some feminists opine there may be a connection between the depiction for violence and sexuality in the media and violence in women's everyday lives but there are other views that the violence in women's lives is presented as a bizarre method. In these ways there remain other women's issues and problems at interpretation level. As a matter of fact to understand the women-media relationship the question should focus on how women can advance their interests as a gender through the media given the different political, religious, cultural, economic and ideological factors towards shaping women's empowerment.

Empowerment of Women

According to the definition put forward by the World Bank it is the process of increasing the capacity of individuals or groups to make effective choices and to transform those choices into desired action and outcomes. If empowerment means power Batiwala (1993) defines power as having two central aspects-controls over resources. If power means control, then empowerment is the process of gaining control. As stated in the Report of the Fourth World Conference on Woman – "The empowerment and autonomy of women and the improvement of women's social, economic and political status is essential for the achievement of both transparent and accountable government and administration and sustainable development in all areas of life." So empowerment of women means ensuring equal power and equal access with men to the increasing range of technological advancement in the changing context of globalization, it means and demands changing policies and legislation along with effective mechanism for implementation of those policies for the benefit of women so that they can exercise their rights and benefit from economic development.

Conclusion

The full participation of women is a prerequisite for governance that is truly democratic. Women continue to be under-represented in formal decision-making structures. Although women are increasingly active in community support systems, gender disparities persist in public positions at all levels: local, national, regional and global. In this regard cohesive measure is to be taken both at national and international level having stringent policy and close monitoring mechanism for effective implementation of women's issues. Otherwise empowerment of women will remain a far cry. In this direction UNDP has a key role to play in promoting legislative, electoral and judicial reform to ensure that women's rights are protected in law and in practice; in enhancing women's participation in the democratic process through decentralization and the bolstering of local governance; in tapping the potential of information and communication technologies as a tool for women's political empowerment; in integrating women's rights into national development strategies; and in bringing women's voices into the national dialogue.

Our government should look into the matter so that the process of economic growth is linked to an expansion in opportunities for women decreasing inequalities. Women's access to basic social services must be increased, education must be made affordable and available, nutrition and health services must be ensured. Women leaders at every level must be supported to build their capacities to function effectively to advance women's interests. Further the media must assume responsibility for their role in forming public opinion, and ensuring that enough space is given to serious women's issues. Women portrayal should reflect the values of gender equality.

REFERENCES

1. Bhasin, K; 1994; 'Women and Communications Alternatives: Hope for the Next Century' in *Media Development*; 2/1994, London; WACC.
2. Burbules, N. C. and C. A. Torres; 2000; *Globalization and Education: Critical Perspectives*, London: Routledge; The introduction available on the web: *http://faculty.ed.uiuc.edu/burbules/ncb/papers/global.html*
3. Castells, M; 2001; 'Information Technology and Global Capitalism' in W. Hutton and A. Giddens (eds.), *On the Edge: Living with Global Capitalism*: London: Vintage.
4. Dutt, R.P; 1949; *India Today* (second edition); Calcutta; Manisha.
5. Fox, J; 2001; *Chomsky and Globalization*; London: Icon Books.
6. Goyal K. A. & P.K. Khicha; 'Globalization of Business: Future Challenges' in *Third Concept - An International Journal of Ideas.*
7. Hirst, P. and G. Thompson; 1996; *Globalization in Question: the International Economy and the Possibilities of Governance*; Cambridge; Polity Press.

8. Michie, J and J. Grieve Smith (eds.); 1995; *Managing the Global Economy*; Oxford; Oxford University Press.

9. Mishra, R; 1999; *Globalization and the Welfare State*; London: Edward Elgar.

10. Romer, Paul M; 1990; 'Endogenous Technological Change', *Journal of Political Economy*; 98(5), pp. 71-102.

11. Shaw, M; 2001; 'Review - Jan Aart Scholte: Globalization - A critical Introduction' in *Milleneum: A Journal of International Studies*; http://www.sussex.ac.uk/Users/hafa3/scholte.htm

12. UNCTAD; 1995-1996; *World Investment Survey for the Years 1994 and 1995*; New York; United Nations.

13. UNCTAD; 1996-1999; *Trade and Development Report for 1996, 1997, 1998, 1999*; New York; United Nations.

14. 'Globalisation, Liberalization and Vulnerability India and Third World' in *Economic and Political Weekly*; 34(45), 6 November, 3219-3230; 1999.

15. 'Globalization's Last Hurrah?' in *Foreign Policy*; January/February 2002; http://66.113.195.237/issue_janfeb_2002/global_index.html

16. 'Globalization: Threat or Opportunity' in *International Monetary Fund*; January 2002; http://www.imf.org/external/np/exr/ib/2000/041200.htm#II

17. 'Human Development Report 2000' in *United Nations Development Programme* (2000); New York; Oxford University Press.

18. 'Women Workers Rights in India: Issues and Strategies- A Reference Guide', *International Labour Organisation*; 1999; New Delhi.

19. 'World Development Report 1998/99: Knowledge for Development' in *World Bank*; [1999, 9 August], Washington; http://www.worldbank.org/wdr/wdr98/contents.htm.

20. Other Sources: Various Websites, Newspapers, Journals and Discussions.

3

Women Empowerment sans Power: Cases from Northeast India

Amiya Kumar Das

Introduction

Women in most Indian society are generally subjected to ill treatment and exploitation, but in north-eastern society the case is different. But it would be wrong to assume that societies in this part of India are free from these incidents. Keeping these things in mind several programmes have been implemented for the sake of women's empowerment but these programmes has hardly helped to elevate their position. In a patriarchal social set up it is difficult to change the social structure but still social engineers are working hard to give justice to the largest minorities in the world in terms of gender. As many feminists have put their argument by saying that family is the starting place where women get exploited and hardly get due respect of their share. This process is being extended to the whole society. As Engels in his seminal work "The Origin of the Family, Private Property and the State" argues that from the primitive period only, women were engaged in productive like making pottery, weaving, gardening and many similar manual works. And this exercise of women contributed a large part in economic life. But with the emergence of private property, men became the master of women and it is this economic oppression that gives rise to the social oppression and other subjugation of women by men. Marxist scholars many often compare women with proletariat and men with bourgeoisie. Whether proletariat will remain in the world or not that is a different question but women will (Engels, 1977).

Similarly feminists argue that women always have secondary position in comparison to men and it is men who always enjoy the privileged position in the society. In the book "The Second Sex", Simone de Beauvoir argues that since long women have in general been forced to occupy a secondary place in the world in relation to men despite the fact that women constitute numerically at least half of the human society (Beauvoir 1989).

So keeping this in mind this paper argues through two case studies in north-eastern part of India that how even after getting access to the economic source women do not have freedom or autonomy. How male folk controls their lives and dictate their agency.

Evidence of the limited control that Indian women exercise over their own lives is increasingly documented. Recent studies underscore their limited control over material and other resources, their restricted access to knowledge and information, their constrained authority to make independent decisions, their enforced lack of physical mobility, and their inability to forge equitable power relationships within families. The role of men as gatekeepers enforcing this status quo is implicitly recognized, and, particularly since the International Conference on Population and Development held in Cairo in 1994, the need to involve men in working for greater gender equity has been widely expressed (Jejeebhoy, 2002).

Micro-credit for women has been a popular empowerment strategy among development agencies since the mid -1980s in the developing countries. It has also been considered an effective vehicle for women's overall development. This is done in terms of small loans, either to individuals or groups. The reason for providing women with loans has been that women are disproportionately represented among the poorest in society and need more help than men in securing sustainable livelihoods. Women are discriminated in the formal labour market and so are usually obliged to seek an income on the margins of the economy, in the informal sector. Women-headed households are on the increase as a result of economic recession, changing labour needs, increasing urbanisation, and the break-up of extended family structures. In some male-headed households, women are now the main source of income. Women-headed households are usually more vulnerable in times of crisis, as they have fewer resources to draw upon (Leach and Sitaram 2002).

Leach and Sitaram argue that most households do not work regularly. Despite this, the major burden of providing food for the family appeared to lie on the women. The men folk mostly agricultural labourers were irregularly employed or unemployed. All children over the age of ten also appeared to do some work. The women were expected to provide not only food for the household but also pay for the husband's 'luxuries' (e.g. cigarettes and alcohol). They usually had to buy small quantities of food daily, often on credit at high interest rates, and could not for the most part take advantage of cheaper options to buy in bulk. Any income earned by the husband would be spent on other items such as school fees, transport, etc. All households had some livestock, which were essential to survival in lean periods (Leach and Sitaram 2002).

From the above study one significant outcome can be well discussed that is in spite of the female members' major contribution to household survival, the women's level of involvement in household decision making was negligible. All important decisions were taken by the husband or closest male relative, while women's daily decisions were restricted to the domestic sphere, in particular what to cook and what food to buy (but husbands always bought the items in the market). Joint decisions might be taken on the education of the children, or on whether a child should be sent to work or married. The women's mobility was also restricted, with even decisions about visits to friends or relatives were made by the husband (Leach and Sitaram 2002).

In India women are defined as inferior, husbands are assumed to 'own' women, and to have the right to dominate them. In-egalitarian gender relations deny women decision making role in family matters; inhibits them from moving about freely, prevent their access to material resources, and expose them to violence in the household. Within this situation of generally limited autonomy, however, sharp cultural and regional differences are found in women's situation and vulnerability (Dyson and Moore,1983).

Empowerment and Women: A Survey

Empowering women by means of credit-based micro-enterprises through the institutional mediation of non-governmental organizations (NGOs), and allowing them to have economic liberty through cooperatives appears to be a well-established developmental belief of the last few decades in India. Sen and Dreze argue that an empowerment of woman is not the issue of women only but it is an integral part of social progress (Sen and Dreze, 1995).

Fernando argues that women's interests are being progressively subordinated to the priorities of development. "Many advocates of empowerment cautiously endorse the articulation of gender interests within the institutional boundaries of mainstream development. In this process ironically, the transformation of empowerment into a subordinate discourse occurs by using its own language and strategies, progressively censoring and muting its radical aspirations. Outcomes in this process are evidence of the neoclassical paradigm's remarkable capacity to accommodate criticisms and challenges without the undermining of its core assumptions and goals". She calls this as the 'subversion' of an emancipatory project (Fernando, 1997 p: 151).

With the help of field research in Bangladesh, she articulates that the success of micro credit programs is facilitated by the very institutions that are considered an obstacle to the empowerment of women. "Women's participation in micro enterprises does not show any signs of creating the new forms of solidarity among women that the advocates of empowerment desire. Instead, women are placed under enormous pressure to maintain existing modes of social relations, on which depend not only the high rates of loan repayments but also the survival of families" (Fernando,1997 p: -152).

In fact, the Oxford English dictionary defines the verb empower as to give some body power or authority to act and to enable. But Empowerment, in general terms, refers to an "institutional environment that enables women to take control over material assets, intellectual resources, and ideology. The material assets over which control can be exercised may be physical, human, or financial, as land, water, forests, people's bodies and labor, money, and access to money. Intellectual resources include knowledge, information, and ideas. Control over ideology signifies the ability to generate, propagate, sustain, and institutionalize specific sets of beliefs, values, attitudes, and behaviour-virtually determining how people perceive and function within a given socio-economic and political environment" (Batliwala, 1994).

The issue of empowerment is taken differently by different authors by saying that it depends on the gender that is male or female. And again in the case of women various other factors are involved regarding the determination of power. And women's access to resources and power is determined by it social and political position in terms of class and caste or ethnicity. Batliwala argues that empowerment "begins not only by recognizing the systemic forces that oppress them, but [by acting] to change existing power relationships. Thus empowerment is a process aimed at changing systemic forces which marginalize women in a given context". Recognition and awareness of these forces that perpetuate women's subordinate position should be followed by a reversal of "values, attitudes, indeed, their entire world view" (Batliwala, 1994) and she suggests that empowerment does not arise from the condition of subjugation and it should be derived from the awareness and consciousness.

As Naila Kabeer suggests "conscientization is an initial step in the struggle through which women define their capacity to define and analyze their subordination, to construct a vision of the kind of world they want, and to act in pursuit of that vision" (Kabeer, 1994). While detailing out the significance of the conscientization approach, Paulo Freire, argued that the "oppressed suffer from a duality which has established itself in their innermost being. They discover that without freedom they cannot exist authentically. Yet, although they desire authentic existence, they fear it. They are at one and the same time themselves and the oppressors whose consciousness they have internalized. The conflict lies in the choice between being wholly themselves or being divided" (Freire, 1968).

If we consider empowerment in terms of this relational dynamic, it becomes the process by which a leader or manager shares his or her power with subordinates. Power, in this context, is interpreted as the possession of formal authority or control over organizational resources (Conger and Kanungo, 1988). The emphasis is primarily on the notion of sharing authority. Burke sees this process of empowerment as representative. "To empower, implies the granting of power delegation of authority" (Burke, 1986)). The Merriam Webster's Dictionary similarly describes the verb to empower as "to authorize or delegate or give legal power to someone". In the management literature, this idea of delegation and the decentralization of decision-making power is central to the empowerment notion (Burke, 1986).

Beteille states that empowerment "means different things to different persons" (Beteille 1999: 589), but he defines as this as empowerment primarily seeks to change society through a rearrangement of power (Beteille, 1999). Where as Dale opines that "Empowerment is a process whereby people acquire more influence over factors that shape their lives. The concept tends to be primarily applied for disadvantaged groups of people, and is usually linked to a vision of more equal living conditions in the society" (Dale 2000: 162). Mohanty expresses his views as "Empowerment involves strengthening the capacity of poor by organising them into informal groups and formal associations and promoting their participation" (Mohanty 2001: 27).

Since last two decades cooperatives are regarded as significant tools to adopt participatory approach for the economic empowerment of women as well as to enhance their social status. Empowerment of women as a goal of development projects and programmes has gained wider acceptance since 1990s (Karl, 1995). Empowerment means not only greater self-confidence, and an inner transformation of one's consciousness that enables one to overcome external barriers to accessing resources or changing traditional ideology. The key elements of empowerment are: power, autonomy and self reliance, entitlement, participation, and process of building awareness and capacity (Panda, 2000).

It is mostly seen that because of the male dominance in every sphere in Indian society even if in the participatory approach women participation are not active and they are being represented by the men-folk. Kabeer talks about the South Asian situation and states that women power over their own life is absent. Based on her analyses of gendered poverty in South Asia, Naila Kabeer analyses power relations over the creation of (dis)empowerment within the relationship of man and women at three levels such as access to power in decision-making agendas, the power over the process of policy-making and the power within, the ideological domination that conceals the reality and pervasiveness of male dominance (Kabeer, 1994).

Empowering the Women: Cases from North-East India

Empowerment of women by means of micro-credit based micro-enterprises is a well-established orthodoxy in the development discourse. In India lot of financial institutions are involved in extending support to women for self sustenance. Similarly Small Industries Development Bank of India (SIDBI) believes that a trained and skilled woman can earn her livelihood and contribute to the country's national income. So, it executes the micro credit system under SIDBI for Micro Credit Scheme by assisting accredited NGOs or Micro Finance Institutions (MFIs) to generate infrastructure facility especially for rural women.

Kshetrimayum in his study in "Imphal, East district of Manipur" on handloom weaving cooperatives has studied 125 handloom cooperative weavers. He tries to question the paradigm of women's empowerment in an era of participatory approach to development. He argues that the agencies for realizing empowerment may be through government organizations like cooperatives. Nevertheless, women are seen as 'targets' to meet programme requirements and goals. Whatever little they may attain, if any, by being part of these organizations and that he calls as 'contextual empowerment'. He says women still suffer isolation, subordination and discrimination in all these models of development. In order to bring rural women empowerment through cooperative, there is an urgent need for revitalization and reorganization of handloom weavers' cooperative societies. The level of members' participation needs to be improved by sensitizing and motivating them before enrolment as members. This should be accompanied by sincere and active efforts from the concerned government agencies (Kshetrimayum, 2008).

Weaving is related to Manipur through the cultural practices. It is very popular household industry in the traditional Meitei world. One of the special features of this industry is that women are the only weavers. Majority of the weavers in the state are self-employed artisans who are carrying on their profession in their own homes with the assistance of their family members in pre-loom and post-loom process. The industry which started to meet limited demands developed as a profession for certain groups of people and the ideas of commercialization for the product generated by these women weavers. These societies have these objectives to safeguard the interests of the weavers from the exploitation and clutches of the middlemen; to supply of raw materials, equipments and other facilities to the members according to their capability of production; to provide finance for promoting industrial activities of the members; to provide technical assistance for raising and maintaining quality in texture, dyeing and production of standard goods; to provide training in new and sophisticated designs which have high demand; and to dispose reasonable wages regularly to the weaving members to enable them to continue in the weaving profession thereby improving their standard of living as well as improving the handloom production. Kshetrimayum raises one question that despite all these, "Are these weavers really empowered?" and he explores through his study. He finds that the cooperative weavers of Manipur who are predominantly women mostly controlled by the men folk. Men mediate between the weaver and donor. One of the objectives of cooperative is to safeguard the interests of the weavers from the exploitation of and clutches of the middlemen. However, the findings of his study shows that almost one-third of the total numbers of weavers still work for the middlemen. This implies that the poor weavers have no alternative other than the middlemen for their survival. This has a highly negative implication on the weavers' socio-economic empowerment (Kshetrimayum, 2008). Large numbers of weavers are not aware of the different schemes for the handloom development project for which men folk get all schemes and they give most of the women members name without asking them. So its shows the lowest level of motivation for empowerment from within.

Mostly government agencies, the financial institutions and NGOs claim empowerment of women through economic assistance. For that they have launched so many schemes and programmes. SIDBI Foundation for Micro Credit Scheme (SFMCs) is one of them. One of the studies conducted by Chakraborty in Guwahati city of Assam, Vijay Nagar area with the self help group called JONAKI (which is a self help group consisting of female member) reveals some interesting issues (Chakraborty, 2008).

The area where she has conducted her field work is a famous handicraft work and credit is mostly sanctioned for this activity. After her study she finds that in spite of the high claims of the government, different financial institutions, media and people in general regarding the successful implementation of SFMC scheme, it is seen from the study that the trend shows something different. She observes that "the success rate of the implementation of the scheme cannot be generalized, because the result is not same everywhere. It is seen that women do not have decision making power in their respective families, because for every word, they wait for their husband's or son's approval i.e. the husband's or son's word is regarded as the final word. Credits received as per the scheme is generally utilized by men folk in the family and not by the women. That is, although the scheme is meant for poor needy women to generate income among them through poultry rearing, weaving, handloom and handicraft, but they are just like sleeping partners in the business because although the loan is being sanctioned in their name, but it is utilized by the men folk of their family, mostly their husbands and sons (Chakraborty, 2008).

From the above two case studies it is well evident that even after having access to economic activities women still depend on the their male counter part for decision making. So it will be difficult to say how they will be empowered only through economic empowerment. Because economic empowerment alone does not guarantee empowerment in all spheres.

Conclusion

This paper has argued that paradoxical nature of empowerment and autonomy in case of women in the north eastern part of India. A powerful discourse has been created on women empowerment through different cooperative schemes and micro credit. But how it looks from the outside is not always true in reality. So there is a need for critical analyses of the political use of 'the empowerment', but we also need to develop a socio-political imaginary that does not repeat these weaknesses and work for empowerment and power of freedom.

Women's economic activities are difficult to compare across countries and within countries over time. There is a cultural variation in interpreting what is productive work depending on the definition given by the particular agency. Much ambiguity has been seen in measurements of women's productive roles that overlap home and market economic activities .It is generally thought that state and civil societies are the two main institutions in empowering women while it is believed that civil society can resist against the ill of state and market. But this has become clear that it is difficult to distinguish the characteristics of state and civil society in the contemporary era.

Can we equate the effects of an empowering process the same as the effects of representation and participation. Empowerment is a psychological construct. This is internal to individuals. Individual power needs are met when they perceive that they have power or when they believe they can adequately cope with events, situations, or the people they confront. On the other hand, individual power needs are disturbed when they feel powerless or when they believe that they are unable to cope with the physical and social demands of the environment. Power in this motivational sense refers to an intrinsic need for self-determination (Deci, 1975) or a belief in personal self-efficacy (Bandura, 1986). From this it can be inferred that empowerment has its base within an actor's motivational outlook.

Although it is believed that the situation of women in North-east part of India is comparatively better than women in other parts of the country. However, this statement can not be rejected fully but at the same time it can not be accepted as it is. From the above case studies we see a different situation. Self-confidence among women can be a component to the empowerment in the real sense as we know that women empowerment only can be achieved if it comes from one's within.

As this paper does not ignore the success story of the cooperative movements and the role of micro credit in giving power to women in certain parts of India, but at the same time we can not generalize this event on an all-India basis. Because this differs from area to area and according to the social values and attitude towards life which also varies from one place to another. Hence there is no certain measurement scale to measure the empowerment of human being including women. It is a non tangible entity; it can not be measured or felt by the other observer. Person can feel within itself. So it is more of a state of mind rather than a state of economic autonomy.

NOTES

I am thankful to Otojit Kshetrimayum and Parna Chakraborty for their valuable input on an earlier version of this paper and for providing some crucial insight from the field.

REFERENCES

1. Bandura, A: 1986; *Social Foundations of Thought and Action: A Social-Cognitive View*; Englewood Cliffs, NJ: Prentice-Hall.
2. Beauvoir, Simone de; 1989; *The Second Sex*; Translated by H. M. Parshley; New York; Vintage Books.
3. Beteille, Andre; 1999; 'Empowerment', in *Economic and Political Weekly*; 34 (11 & 12): 589-97.
4. Burke, W; 1986; 'Leadership as Empowering Others', in S. Srivastra (ed.), *Executive Power;* (pp. 51-77); San Francisco; Jossey-Bass.
5. Chakraborty, Parna; 2008; *Role of Small Industries Development Bank of India in Socio Economic Empowerment of Women: A study of Vijay Nagar Area of Kamrup District, Assam;* Project Report submitted in the Department of Sociology, Tezpur University, Assam.
6. Conger, Jay A. & Rabindra N. Kanungo; 1988; 'The Empowerment Process: Integrating Theory and Practice', in *The Academy of Management Review;* Vol. 13, No. 3 pp. 471- 482.
7. Dale, Reider; 2000; *Organisations and Development: Strategies, Structures and Process.*
8. Deci, E. L; 1975; *Intrinsic Motivation;* New York; Plenum.
9. Dyson, Tim and Mick Moore; 1983; 'On kinship Structure, Female Autonomy and Demographic Behaviour in India', in *Population and Development Review;* 9(1): 35-60.
10. Engels, Frederick; 1977; *The Origin of the Family, Private Property and the State;* Moscow; Progress Publishers.
11. Fernando, Jude L; 1997; 'Non-governmental Organizations, Micro-Credit, and Empowerment of Women', in *Annals of the American Academy of Political and Social Science;* Vol. 554, pp. 150-177, Sage Publication.
12. Jejeebhoy, Shireen J; 2002; 'Convergence and Divergence in Spouses' Perspectives on Women's Autonomy', in *Rural India Studies in Family Planning;* Vol. 33, No. 4 (Dec., 2002), pp. 299-308.
13. Kabeer, N; 1994; *Reversed Realities: Gender Hierarchies in Development Thought;* London; Verso.
14. Karl, M; 1995; *Women and Empowerment: Participation and Decision Making;* London; Zed Books.

15. Kshetrimayum, Otoji; 2008; 'Rethinking Cooperatives in Rural Development: A Case Study of Handloom Weaving Cooperatives in Manipur', Paper presented in the National seminar on *Revitilising Rural Institutes: Problems and Prognosis* organised by National Council of Rural Institutes (NCRI), at Gandhi Darshan and Smriti, New Delhi on 15 and 16 March 2008.

16. Leach, Fiona and Shashikala Sitaram; 2002; 'Microfinance and Women's Empowerment: A Lesson from India', in *Development in Practice*; Volume 12, Number 5.

17. Mohanty, M; 2001; 'On the Concept of Empowerment', in D.K. SinghaRoy (ed.), *Social Development and the Empowerment of Marginalised Groups: Perspective and Strategies*; (22-30). New Delhi; Sage Publications.

18. Panda, S. M; 2000; 'Women's Empowerment through NGO Intervention.: A Framework for Assessment', in *Social Change*; Vol. 30. Nos. 3& 4.

19. Paulo, Freire; 1968; *Pedagogy of the Oppressed*; New York; Seasbury Press.

20. Sen, Amartya & Jean Dreze; 1999; *India Economic Development and Social Opportunity;* New Delhi; Oxford University Press.

21. Srilatha, Batliwala; 1994; 'Meaning of Empowerment: New Concepts, Form, Action', in Gita Sen, Adrienne Germaine, and Lincoln Chen (ed.), *Population Policies Reconsidered: Health Empowerment and Rights;* Cambridge; Harvard University Press.

4

Gender Conflict: Whose End Does It Serve?

Chandan Debnath

"We are all pencils in the hand of God writing love letters to the world."

- *Mother Theresa*

Freedom, identity and independence are cherished by every heart. Infringement in any form is despised and the natural response is to protect them in the face of extreme adversity. Meaning of the above words do not change either in the context of gender, race, nationality or religion. Freedom cannot mean something to a citizen of first world and something different for a person living in the third world. Attempts at attributing different meanings to the innate needs of men based on gender can best be described with the word, 'being biased'. Biasness is a behavioural outcome which lies beyond rational explanations or logical arguments. It is just a reflection of weakness that has crept into ones personality, making him or her a hallowed entity, devoid of constructive purpose. Biasness encourages finding excuses for upholding puffed up egos, baseless superiority or explores means to protect self-interest at the cost of the other. If this observation is false, than how else can one define or articulate gender biasness?

The English proverb 'behind every successful man there

is a women' is a complete truth and needs no authentication or acknowledgement from the men folk. Even if men shy from acknowledging the same, true to our hearts we are aware that without their contribution each of us stands incomplete by all respects. Now let me put it the other way, 'behind every successful woman there is man'. Well in principle, it is a bit difficult to accord complete acceptance, though equally valid and true in all respects. The obvious reason being biasness that superficially describes men superior to women. However as conscientious being we are aware that the reciprocal relationship between the genders cannot be either undermined or overstated in the making of a society and all its constituent elements that forms a part of the society. Undermining or overstating in the said context can best be described as plain biasness. Men and women play a complimentary role in furtherance of social goal of well-being vide peace, progress and prosperity.

Another aspect which runs parallel to the need for freedom and independence is the universal urge for betterment in all facets of socio-economic and cultural life. In this context, I understand the urge for betterment as a synonym for growth and development. The word development might connote different meanings to varied users. For an economist development means rise in per-capita income, savings and investment, GDP, etc. A sociologist measures the impact of development relating it to levels of social cohesiveness that a society enjoys. An anthropologist visualizes development by measuring the changes in human evolution with relation to his/her environment so on and so forth. These diverse meanings of development when tied together convey the ultimate human desire for betterment and meaningful existence. Men is a product of his/ her environment and thus one cannot find a uniform and precise explanation of the term 'meaningful existence' but its influence as a guiding force cannot be negated. Anthropologists have identified modernization as human progress from stages such as: hunter–gatherer or foraging, horticultural, agricultural or agrarian, and so on (Walker). Each of this stage represented a distinct mile stone collectively reached irrespective of gender breakup.

In the context of defining the role of women in development

feminist have argued for giving greater place to women in the organization of social and production relations, family structure, patterns of property ownership, and forms of work and production. Whatever be the arguments the end purpose is quite cogent, that is development activities worldwide shall fail to deliver its mission if women remain out of its purview in areas of planning, organizing, decision making and overall participation. Any development structure and form denying ample and equal space to women runs the risk of deformities and internal contradictions and thus nullifying the very purpose of development. Leaving women outside the development matrix simply malnourishes the effectiveness of development, resulting in the deformed growth of the society. In the process such biasness promotes absurd reasons to perpetuate violence against women, carry on with exploitation and deprive them the right of being heard and respected. If one is to develop a compendium listing all violations against women well, it will ever remain in complete, as women in underdeveloped and developing societies everyday day is confronted with new forms of violence that question their basic dignity as human beings.

All said and done, it is equally true that erudite scholarships and lengthy polemics by itself shall not do any good in empowering the fair gender or bestow to them their rights. Take the issue of reservation for women in parliament, God best knows when it shall see the light of the day. Contemplating on the issue I often fail to understand, what is that which keeps our Hon'ble Members of Parliament to build a consensus on the issue. After all the reservation policy does not call for 100% reservation, for men to be apprehensive off. Its just demands 33.33% space for women in the Parliament and allow them an opportunity to work for nation building in that capacity. Further their entry to parliament shall be guided by the best tradition of democracy as entry is decided by ballots not on whims and fancy. So its time our male dominated parliament and state legislature en-mass lend their support to 'Women Reservation Bill' without a second thought. I wish in the near future our parliament will reverberate with words Long Live Women Bill, Zindabad and by doing so men apart from proving their chivalry (though uncalled for as it is a legitimate right for half a billion of Indian population) will give the clear message 'well we acknowledge that nation building is incomplete without women playing a decisive part in it.

Tracing the Origins of Discrimination

Since the late 1960s feminist social scientist have been collecting empirical evidence that women were either ignored from the development process, or assigned roles which did not allow them to benefit from the development process like their male counterparts. Women were relegated a lower status and the dominant explanation of the time was, issue of biological determinism which saw man different from a women in terms of physical structure, strength and appearance. Agreeing to the above submission I would like to stress more on the issue of physical strength which had been instrumental in propagating the issue of gender divide over the ages. Physical power indicates strength and stamina aimed at ensuring submission of the opponent. To substantiate with examples, let's begin with the hunting expeditions of our distant forefathers in the prehistoric period. Chasing wild beast required stamina and women definitely could not match their male partners in this act. Being comparatively weak in this front it might have triggered beliefs of superior vs the inferior, subsequently paving the way for gender discrimination in manifold facets. Further trying to establish a relation for gender inequities, one can trace its beginning as an outcome of numerous wars man have staged for gaining political or economic dominance or at times simply satisfy the bloody hungry thirst of wily tyrants, emperors who found pleasure in pain. History exemplifies wars as exclusive domain of man and women's roles was limited to sitting back at home and wait patiently for the outcome of all such exercise of human disaster carried with or without a cause. Being physically weak compared to men they traditionally had no role in military expeditions and men saw them as an additional burden to cater apart from being engaged in military strategies. Since women were dependent on men for protection during aggression and conflicts; this dependency could have been instrumental for male dominating society according non equal position to women compared to men. This initial perception over the ages found way in the cultural practices of communities to consider the status of women in the societal hierarchy lower to that of man. In the early 1970s, British feminist Sociologist Ann Oakley (1972) expressed this as a distinction between sex and gender: "Sex as word refers to the biological differences between male and female, the visible difference in genitalia, the related difference in procreative function. Gender however is a matter of culture: it refers to classifications such as masculine and feminine". The change of terminology from sex as a determinism to gender however could achieve little vis-à-vis improving the status of women. There is no doubt that Oakley's definition was an important innovation of the time arguing against discrimination primarily on the ground of determinism by sex. However the cultural connotations articulated through the usage of the word 'gender' could not achieve the goals of gender mainstreaming. The crucial question which comes to ones mind is what is gender 'mainstreaming'.

'Gender mainstreaming' was defined by the United Nations Economic and Social Council in 1997 as 'a strategy for making women's as well as men's concerns and experiences an integral dimension of the policies and programmes in political, economic and societal spheres so that, women and men benefit equally and inequality is not perpetuated.' The relative status of men and women; the interaction between gender and race, class and ethnicity and questi New Delhi-ons of rights, control, ownership, power and voice all have a critical impact on the success and sustainability of every development intervention. In practice, gender mainstreaming means identifying gaps in gender equality and addressing them in the right perspective.

Despite good intentions and some real progress, the development community, UNDP included, believes that efforts are still falling short in respect of materializing its goals. Some of the problem areas as identified in the UN Secretary-General's Review and Appraisal of the Implementation of the Beijing Platform for Action include the lack of accountability mechanisms; insufficiency of resources; lack of priorities concerning planning for female gender such as health and education, and overall absence of a strong political commitment in the above direction. The Beijing Platform identifies key area that needs to be targeted in order achieve the developmental goals as identified by world body. The need to dedicate collective efforts can be envisaged from Kemal Dervis own words: *"As we move forward with the implementation of the Millennium Development Goals (MDGs), it is important that we are fully committed to investing in policies and programmes that empower women and promote gender equality." – Kemal Dervis, UNDP Administrator, 6 Sept. 2005. One of the most serious inhumane treatments meted out to women is violence of all sorts that are directed at them and UNDP gives a clarion call to take up this issue as priority. The reason being women subjected with violence find little reason to contribute to the growth and development of the society in the best of their capability. Citing UNDP report it becomes apparent that societies and communities world wide has to make concerted efforts in ending violence against women and girls and the same is quoted verbatim.* "A few months from now in July 2007, we will pass the halfway point on our timeline for achieving the Millennium Development Goals (MDGs). As that date approaches, we should pause and take stock of the impediments we still need to overcome to reach our promised targets by 2015. One obvious barrier to the MDGs is violence against women". In the light of the above the Human Development Mandate reflected in the Millennium Developmental Goals calls for the following:

1. Ensure women are afforded the same freedoms and opportunities as men. In the absence of commitment it shall be impossible to promote equality where one in every three women world wide are tormented in her lifetime, regardless of her culture, religion, socio-economic class or education level.

2. Distance from cultural beliefs that overtly and covertly encourage battering and violence or best remain a mute spectator to the scepter of violence such as dowry deaths, rape, honor killings, coerced marriages, abortion of girl child, abuse of the female child etc.

3. Find no reasons to justify that in times of crisis women are

the natural victims and which though regrettable is unavoidable. This is a fallacious thinking and needs correction. Such an attitude shall only contribute to the pandemic of violence and provide impunity for perpetrators to further silence the survivors. More generally, we have to accept the truth that repression of women and their rights adds to unequal social structures and the lack of freedom retards endeavors centered at human development.

4. Recognize the fact that violence against women is a result of historically unequal power relations between men and women resulting in subordination and discrimination. Violation of women's human rights impedes human development for all. The present needs to address the issue in the right perspectives so that women enjoy their legitimate rights that one constituent of human population have deliberately denied to them.

Women and Development

Amartya Sen (1999) in his seminal work 'Development as Freedom' states the core goal of development must be social well being of the masses and promotion of freedom. "Freedoms," he argues, "are not only the primary ends of development, they are also among its principal means." Therefore development should be viewed as a process of expanding freedoms. "If freedom is what development advances, then there is a major argument for concentrating on that overarching objective, rather than on some particular means, or some chosen list of instruments". To achieve development, he argues, requires the removal of poverty, tyranny, lack of economic opportunities, social deprivation, neglect of public services, and the machinery of repression. This is indeed a crucial aspect of 'development as freedom'.

The Nobel laureate's articulations testify the premise on which the paper is framed i.e. the inherent desire for freedom and independence against all sorts of inequities. Highlighting that purpose of development is removal of un-freedoms which is pregnant with meanings in the context of gender inequities and one has to unfold them to understand its significance. The un-freedoms have been explained vide the usage of the words poverty, tyranny, deprivation, marginalization, repression etc. Rampant existence of the same in our society needs no referencing in the context of women's violation of rights. One shall find it difficult to disagree that dowry and the consequent ills associated with it exist in our society. There is a hypocrisy that follows this practice i.e., pretending to be against dowry but yet find reasons to practice it in some form or other. If I am permitted I shall call it the ignominy of seeking forced gifts from the opposite sex. Can anything be more humiliating to a male? In seeking gifts where does his so called male ego hide? How does he justify his great acts of chivalry that he loves to garrulously promote himself at the expense of the opposite gender. Inability to find answers to these questions exhibits ones hollowness and lack of principles. That is why I term it hypocrisy. I recollect as child I saw mother blow the smoky chullah day in and day out that too, when alternative fuel was available in our town. Often thinking that cooking with LPG was a status symbol I used to ask my mother to use the same in our kitchen. Many a times she used to remain silent to my persistence until one day she told me '*Gas aar dam bishi todair poralekha Khoti hobai*' translated from Bengali it means (Gas is expensive buying will upset the budget of your education). To be very candid I could not get the meaning of her words then or appreciate her sacrifice by opting for the chullah instead of the comforts allowed by cooking with LPG. Years latter visualizing my mother cooking in small *Rasoi Ghar* 6ft by 5ft full of white smoke (especially during monsoon when the wood used to be wet) fills my heart with remorse.

The point I wish to emphasise is millions of housewives in our country choke themselves in the slow poisonous gas rather than upset the family budget using LPG. Added to it if the food cooked falls short of the general expectations barring exceptions she is abused either verbally or physically or in extreme cases both irrespective of her status in the family as a mother, sister, spouse, daughter-in-law etc. The irony is that she has bear up all this either to prove: her respect for elders and family norms (*parampara*), sense of belongingness, or in the name of upholding family honor. A women's injury gets compounded when she is tormented by another woman (may be mother-in-law, mistress of the house, sister in-law). This is a stark reality that exists in many of the Indian households irrespective of religion, class and caste. Gaurang Bhatt's (2004) paper, presented on the eve of Women's International Day shall be classic reading for those who fail to appreciate the position of women: "The generosity of the female gamete is the birth of gender and proof of greater nobility by choice. All of us male and female get half our genes from the father and half from our mother, but we get our mitochondria and mitochondrial genes entirely and solely from our mothers. These maternal organelles allow us to consume oxygen and generate energy. The '*Praana*' that gives us our '*Jiva*' is exclusively maternal". Presenting the position of women she questions the basic cultural beliefs and practices that have been instrumental in creating a sense of insecurity amongst women.

There is another interesting facet that can be brought in to the discussion and which is the concept of 'colour matching'. I find this concept a dominating issue concerning arranged weddings. As a preference every prospective bridegroom wishes to get a bride fair enough to be termed 'angel of the house' as portrayed in Charlotte Bronte's novel "Jane Eyre". The woman is rarely given any scope to express her colour preferences vis-à-vis the groom but she can be screened out of process because of her complexion. The mental trauma a woman has to face either on being rejected on the grounds of complexion or having to live with a partner who is not her first choice is definitely a very frustrating experience and she has bear up everything because the male society has forced upon her the unquestionable acceptance of male dictates. Of course things are changing thanks to women empowerment but a lot needs to be achieved. The internal pain and conflict that a woman experience can be best visualized in the reflections of *Ernestine Rose* **a women activist (1810 – 1892)** "Away with that folly that her rights would be detrimental to her character - that if she were recognized as the equal to a man she would cease to be a woman!" "But it will be said that the husband provides for the wife, or in other words, he feeds, clothes and shelters her! I wish I had the power to make every one before me fully realize the degradation contained in that idea". On women's participation in government she had this say, "But say some, would you expose woman to the contact of rough, rude, drinking, swearing, fighting men at the ballot box? What a humiliating confession lies in this plea for keeping woman in the background!" On the issue of child upbringing her view is, "Fathers like to have children good-natured, well-behaved, and comfortable, but how to put them in that desirable condition is out of their philosophy" Reflecting on the position of women in many families she says "From the cradle to the grave she is subject to the power and control of man. Father, guardian, or husband, one conveys her like some piece of merchandise over to the other".

Concerning aspects of gaining trust or on matters of rights over children she reflects the reality as "If they are unsuccessful in married life, who suffers more the bitter consequences of poverty than the wife? But if successful, she has not a dollar to call her own." In case of separation, why should the children be taken from the protecting care of the mother? Who has a better right to them than she? How much do fathers generally do towards bringing them up? It is high time to compel man by the might of right to give woman her political, legal and social rights. She will find her own sphere in accordance with her capacities, powers and tastes; and yet she will be woman still". The bringing up and safety of the children are left with the mother, and safe they are in her hands. But a few hundred or thousand dollars can not be in trusted with her!" Exposing the double standards which are reflected by the male ego her understanding is 'Much is said about the burdens and responsibilities of married men. Responsibilities indeed there are, if they but felt them: but as to burdens what are they?" Even the judiciary often seems to suffer from biases and Christina substantiates this with her own account, "Not long ago, I saw an account of two offenders, brought before a Justice of New York. One was charged with stealing a pair of boots, for which offense he was sentenced to six months' imprisonment; the other crime was assault and battery upon his wife; he was let off with a reprimand by the judge!" The male prejudice is finely projected by her as, "The main cause is a pernicious falsehood propagated against her being, namely that she is inferior by her nature. Inferior in what? What has man ever done that woman, under the same advantages could not do?" Deliberating on many other problems that women face in the society she with a tinge of bitterness comments, "When the husband dies poor, to be sure no guardian is required, and the children are left for the mother to care and toil for, as best she may. But when anything is left for their maintenance, then it must be placed in the hands of strangers for safekeeping!" Contemplating on the plight of millions of women across the globe she calls upon one and all to introspect and find answers, "Where again I ask is the result of those noble achievements, when woman, aye, one half of the nation, is deprived of her rights: Has woman, then been idle during the contest between 'right and might'? Will you tell us that women have no Newton's, Shakespeare's and Byron's?"

We may find it difficult to accept all her view points. The difference in understanding could be because of our background, social status, education etc,. But if we take a moment and ponder seriously than it will dawn on us that woman especially from underprivileged communities continually experience all that *Ernestine Rose has said and projected years ago. The purpose of quoting her is not make generalizations that things remained the same even after two centuries but only draw attention to women in the 21st century who still have to live with idiosyncrasies, and hypocrisies that blocks her path from gaining freedom and emancipation.*

Ordinary Women as Makers of History

This phrase has been borrowed from Bijal Dwivedi (2001) and the central point reiterates that women should not be construed as a burden but rather as equal and effective partners in the making of a society and in the process set the ball rolling in undoing the history that is smudged with gender deprivation, inequities and other forms of injustice perpetrated deliberately and non-deliberately against women. The life of these great women is an open book for all those who believe that women are a inferior community and from them learn lessons of love, peace, understanding, equality, mutual respect, sacrifice, professionalism, leadership, statesmanship, dedication, commitment, loyalty, patriotism and nation building. Eve (first women as per Christian mythology), Gargi (great Sanskrit exponent), Florence Nightingale, Rani of Janshi, Indira Gandhi, Diana - princess of Wales, Helen Keller (the woman who overcame barriers of deafness and blindness), Dame - Agatha Christie (The Mystery Novelist), Agnes Gonxha Bojaxhiu (popular known to world as Mother Teressa, Missionary of the poor) MarieCurie, Emily Dickinson (poet) Irom Sharmila (Human Right Activist), Rani Gaidiliniu (Freedom Fighter), Kalpana Chawla (Astronaut), Sunita Willams (Astronuat), Virginia Woolf (British Feminist), Aung San Suu Kyi (Nobel Laureate for Peace), Jane Austin (Novelist), Elanor Roosevelt (Rights Activist), Golda Meir (First Israeli Women Prime Minister), Rosa Luxemburg (Revolutionary Leader), Wangari Maathai (Nobel Laurete), LKG and UKG Teachers' (who have always been women imparting the first crucial knowledge) and of course the mothers who are best managers and leaders in their own capacity.

In Hindu scriptures most of the deities represent the female gender and they are revered for bestowing wealth, power, protection, learning, freedom from diseases, sustenance and in the same context mind you the most feared deities are *Sani* (Saturn) and *Yama* (God of death) incidentally both males from whom always safe distance is sought. Well if this is true then is it prudent to still uphold arguments concerning the superiority of male gender. Putting it in a lighter note, I would say if we continue to violate women's right than lets be sure we are bound to incur the wrath all our venerated deities.

The benefits of technology and science have been innumerable. We are now witnessing global communication at a pace previously unimaginable. New vistas have been opened for humanity; to name a few: an extended life span, increased educational and cultural opportunities, political and economic empowerment, and exploration of life beyond planet earth. Together with these advancements, however, new challenges confront us regarding the dignity of women and child. One segment of the human population cannot benefit at the cost of the others. Development being a collective exercise of human betterment will not find meaning in the context of gender dominance/discrimination. The practice and belief dominance have to make way for partnership, involving and empowering either sexes to play their unique roles. In this new millennium women have a unique role to play in the care of the human person and in the transformation of society, so as to provide a more congenial setting for human flourishing. Women have always been in the vanguard of civilization, playing their varied roles as daughters, sisters, spouse, and mother which need appreciation and acknowledgement. The Beijing Conference 2000 has identified some areas that call for greater attention and larger women participation such as: Environment, Health, Poverty, Peace, Education, Human Rights, and Political empowerment. The rational being, as these issues concerns human race obstructing one segment of the human population from effectively contributing to it will contribute to a concept of developmental blackhole.

Discrimination shall only undermine the common journey of men and women as higher beings inhabiting this beautiful planet. The need of the hour is not perpetuating gender conflict but building partnership as expected by the Cosmic being. Facilitating this partnership calls for a change of attitude and realization i.e., women are not 'Symbols of Sacrifice' nor 'Sacrificial Lambs' but our equal half capable of performing in the same capacity as men.

REFERENCES

1. Bhatt, Gaurang; 2004; *Females: Superior by Choice, Design and Default;* Source: www.boloji.com/rt2/rt111.htm
2. Dwivedi, Bijal; 2001; Source: www. boloji.com/ writers/bijal.htm
3. Goyal, Sangeeta; *How to be a Woman, though a Human; Source*: www.boloji.com/rt2/rt111.htm
4. Madhur, Meenakshi; 2001; *Women – Symbols of Sacrifice or Sacrificial Lambs;* Source: www. Boloji.com/ writers/mMeenakshi madhur.htm
5. Pharr, Suzanne; *Divisions that Kill: The Enemy Without and Within;* Source: http://feminism.eserver.org/theory/papers/ htm.

6. Simons, Margaret A; 1999; *Behaviour and the Second Sex*; Rowman & Littlefield Publishers, Inc with Sylvie Le Bon de Beauvoir - http://www.amazon.com/ Beauvoir - Second-Sex-Feminism - Existentialism/dp/0847692566

7. Wallace, Heather E; *Woman's Education According to Rousseau and Wollstonecraft;* source: http://feminism.eserver.org/theory/papers/

8. http://quotations.about.com/od/morepeople/a/woman3.htm.

9. http://www.undp.org/women/mainstream/ retrieved 12/05/07

10. http://www.fahamu.org/downloads/DevelopmentasFreedom.pdf, retrieved on 12/05/07

11. http://www.undp.org/women/, retrieved on 16/05/07

12. http://content.undp.org/go/newsroom/march-2007/international-womens-day-statement-dervis-20070308.en

5

The Naga Marriage

Monalisa Changkija

[*Today the Naga marriage is an interesting study of a tribal society in transition into a form of modernism, the characters, the contents and contours of which is not quite clear at this point of time. The dynamics of marriage is generally a mirror of the dynamics of any society and the Naga marriage, which is a product of the patriarchal Naga society, definitely operates along patriarchal norms and reflects it.*]

Now there are certain things we need to be very clear about the realities of the Naga marriage. For one, there is no one or two types of Naga marriages but as many as there are Naga marriages and unless anyone has devoted a good amount of time and energy studying them from the anthropological, sociological or whatever perspective it is difficult to even broadly categorize the Naga marriage. And as I have not made any such study I really cannot and do not speak with any authority on the subject but I will try to give a fair picture of the reality of the Naga marriage, let us say from empirical evidence.

Two, we must have a fair idea about the Naga marriage in traditional Naga society to be able to arrive at some conclusion about the changes that have occurred in the institution of marriage in today's modern Naga society. Read any number of books on Naga traditional society, especially on social norms, you will notice the unequal status and position of women however politically correctly they have been written. The unequal status and position of women in Naga traditional society is nothing but a natural corollary of the patriarchal system and values upon which our society, irrespective of tribe, is founded. Consequently, the traditional Naga marriage was, without exception, a totally unequal one, where the role of the wife is taken for granted as subservient. And this is reflected in the larger social context, not only in the equations of the traditional Naga marriage but also in the dynamics of the larger social life of Naga society. So we had women not only serving and obeying but also excluded from the decision-making process in the social, religious, political and cultural spheres of Naga society. At this point, one wonders how traditional Naga society is sometimes perceived to have had the 'purest' form of democracy.

Three, let us also study the impact of the trappings of modernism such as education and its concomitants on the dynamics of marriage and whether they reiterate the patriarchal values and mindsets or weaken them. Much as women tend to have a very romantic notion about marriage, the fact of the matter is that in any patriarchal society marriage is an unequal contract simply because it is a contract between a male and a female, who do not have equal status and position in society. So any relationship between two 'unequal' partners cannot be 'equal'. A relationship such as marriage depends on either of the partners inevitably having to 'give in' more often than not for it to be 'successful'. By and large, women inevitably tend to 'give in' in such relationships due to varied and various factors and Naga marriage is more the norm in this kind of relationship than the exception.

How then is the modern Naga marriage different from that of traditional Naga society?

Firstly, let us have no illusions that all the factors that led to the union of two families or clans, through the institution of marriage do not persist today, albeit in a very different avatar. But today marriages are more the decision and/or choice of individual couples and such choices are more the norm than the exception. This definitely is the result of modern education and the exposure to a global worldview, especially that of individual rights and liberties. The increase in inter-tribal and inter-community marriages amongst us is actually one of the happiest results of modern education and its concomitants, especially because such marriages result in rationalizing our traditionally held biases and prejudices, or at least help us to minimize them. But I am not sure how much of this is a result of the spread of Christianity because this religion too reinforces all patriarchal systems and values.

Naga marriage today must also be seen in the context of the dynamics of the market. As we increasingly absorb, and at the same time get absorbed into, the process of globalization, all human relationships are also undergoing changes from their traditional avatars. The fact is today the market dictates and demands a very different kind of human relationship and to survive in today's markets, we need to adapt to the kind of relationship the market demands and dictates. In the process human beings and human relationships are constrained to become subservient to the market but the market does not do away with the patriarchal systems and values, in fact, it further reinforces them. In the new market order, the unequal status and position of women are further underlined and their subservient role further accentuated. Only the difference now is that women are encouraged and facilitated to come out of the four-walls of the house (or should that be the four walls of the kitchen?), acquire education and expertise and hone their skills to be better qualified to tend to the market's demands and dictates. At the same time, women also have to don on the mantle of homemaker and motherhood. If traditional society had heaped upon women all responsibilities but very little or no rights, the modern market has trebled that. Today modern women, more so the Naga women, is stretched and stressed to her limits rushing around to meet the demands of both the market and the home with very little say in both the market and the home but unfortunately a myth is created about her 'educated and empowered' status and position and she is yet to see her reality for exactly what it is.

So then, as much as the Naga women is stretched and stressed, so is the Naga marriage. To be sure, today the Naga wife has a lot more to say in a lot of the decision-making process in her marital family/home. In fact, it has become more convenient for the Naga husband to leave the family/home's decision making to his wife. This is due to several factors. Today more Naga wives have a higher level of educational qualifications than their husbands, which also means they are bringing home a bigger pay packet. Even Naga wives who do not have salaried jobs earn through their entrepreneurial skills in various factors. This empowers them to take their rightful share in the decision-making process in the family/home. Today most Naga husbands also have/had mothers, who are/were educated and are/were working or have worked outside the home, as also earning/earned through entrepreneurial businesses and or in the private sector. Hence today Naga husbands are learning not to be as contemptuous about their wives' decision-making abilities, as perhaps a generation of Naga males before them. Naga men with daughters also tend to have a very different worldview and I need not elaborate why.

But all this doesn't mean that Naga women have attained equality in today's Naga marriage simply because our society and our males have not abandoned the foundation and roots of our existence – patriarchy. However educated, exposed and enlightened, Naga men and Naga society have not abandoned our patriarchal core. Now, as far as Naga women are concerned, this means that they have to meet the demands and dictates of both traditional Naga society as well as that of the modern market. The load on the back of the Naga women is doubled as today the Naga married woman has to not only meet the demands of the family/home, as a wife and a mother, but also the dictates and obligations of her responsibilities as a daughter, daughter-in-law, sister, sister-in-law, etc., and at the same time the demands and dictates of her job/career/profession. All these also translate into her heavier social responsibilities, which also extract a not-so-small physical, mental, psychological and financial pound of flesh.

Now the other issue we need to look at vis-à-vis the Naga marriage is the exact status of the Naga wife's economic empowerment. Education and academic qualifications are means of empowerment, not empowerment *per se*. Education and academic qualifications, acquiring expertise, skills, in whatever field, and honing them provides a woman a level playing field in the market and to some extent at home but does not actually empower her as a person, not when she is confined to the rules of a patriarchal value-system and must abide by them, as also cooperate with them. For all the trappings of modernism, the Naga wife is a Naga woman, not yet a Naga person. I hope you will discern the difference. Under the circumstances, let us try to study the Naga wife's exact economic empowerment status. Bringing home a huge pay packet or earning a huge profit doesn't make anyone economically empowered. We have to look at economic empowerment also from the perspective of spending and saving. So how much is the Naga wife spending and how much is she saving? What is she spending on? What is she saving? How much of what she earns, spends and saves is translating into facilitating her to be recognized as a person in her own right in the familial, social, societal, economic, political and religious spheres of the Naga society? After all, today it is the investor, who calls the shots. It is only after we find ways and means to calculate this we can talk about Naga women's economic empowerment. Look at it from this perspective, even if a Naga wife earns a lot of money, if she has to spend all of that on her home/family and can save nothing, she is still back to square one – a totally de-franchised and de-empowered woman – simply because she would have to depend on someone else in the event of sickness, destitution, abandonment and so many other evils that befall on women in any 'self-respecting' patriarchal society.

This now brings us to the issue of inheritance. Today Naga fathers are giving their acquired movable and immovable property (including land) to their daughters, either during their lifetime or have written wills to that effect. Inarguably, the best gift parents are giving their daughters is education, which has enabled Naga women to acquire their own movable and immovable property. This actually is also another very crucial factor in the Naga wife today having a lot more share in the decision-making process in her marital family/home. However, because Naga society has not abandoned the patriarchal norms of inheritance, proprietorship/ownership, etc., of movable and immovable property, and at the same time, with life in the market becoming more 'brutish' very dark zones of the Naga wife's economic status have emerged. If a Naga man does not gift his daughter movable and immovable property, she is already de-franchised in terms of inheritance. If Naga man does not leave behind any movable and immovable property to his wife, the same daughter is doubly de-franchised in terms of inheritance. Now even if a Naga woman acquires movable and immovable property and male members of her family/families take them away, in the event of abandonment, destitution, divorce and death, her de-enfranchisement is complete. Let's also look at the Naga wife's economic empowerment from this perspective – she first lives in her father's house/home, then in her husband's and finally in her son's house/home, and in all of them she invests physically, mentally, psychologically and financially but gets no returns.

Whether in a traditional or modern Naga society, Naga marriage totally subverts the Naga woman's personhood and that is generally her reality even in the larger context of the society. You have not far to look at but at our political, economic, social, religious, and now even in our development processes. Naga woman, whatever her educational qualifications, her status, her intelligence, talents and all other attributes, still cooks and serves tea and meals to males when they do the decision-making.

Now all this is not to say Naga woman should not acquire education and arm themselves to participate in the dynamics of the market or revert back to the days of their grandmothers. This is also not to say that all Naga marriages are relationships of abject bondage. After all, any marriage depends on so many factors, especially that of mindsets, attitudes and maturity. What I am underscoring is the need to scrutinize how much of the fundamentals of the Naga marriage have changed and how much have remained unchanged, and in which areas and aspects. I am also underscoring the need to scrutinize the exact realities of the Naga marriage so that like any other institution, so crucial for human survival, the Naga marriage too is de-constructed where and when need, and re-constructed where and when necessary, as also transformed and evolved into more sensitized and productive institution keeping pace with the requirements of the times. It is after all the Naga marriage from where all changes, so direly needed in our society, would germinate.

I still firmly maintain that the load on the back of the Naga woman is doubled in today's Naga marriage and I have just a few pointers today but it is for each of you to decide the exact reality of today's Naga marriage and juxtapose it against the traditional Naga marriage and arrive at your own conclusions.

By no means is what I have said today the last word on the Naga marriage, in fact, it is the first word, so to speak. There are many aspects of the Naga marriage I have not touched such as domestic violence, marital rape, sharing/non-sharing of kitchen expenses, shouldering the burden of children's education – financially and otherwise –, infidelity, alcoholism, in-laws' interference, customary laws and traditions that act as roadblocks towards Naga marriage growing into a modern institution that brings out the best in the family and consequently in society, inability or unwillingness of especially males to prioritize their marital and paternal families/homes, etc.

6

Changing Gender Equity and Status Achievement

Visakhonu Hibo

[Men for the field and women for the hearth,
Man for the sword and for the needle she,
Man with the head and woman with the heart,
Men to command and women to obey,
All else confusion

- *Lord Alfred Tennyson*]

Mindsets and pre-conceived notions about gender issues generally start with such attitudes without opening up of one's mind. Any attempt to conduct women studies may also provoke one's mind to two opposite ends. One thought can be the Feminist/ Activist approach which is highly emotive and subjective. And the other is the Academic approach which is supposed to be highly objective and neutral. Gender studies and gender analysis made by academicians must, therefore, be neutral and concepts used must be very clear.

With this belief, the concepts of "Sex versus Gender" is sought to be explained. One's sex is primarily a biological quality, while one's gender is formed largely (but not entirely) by the cultural forces we experience through socialization from infancy on (Connell, 1995).

Sex refers to the biological differences between a male and a female, including the primary sex characteristics that are present at birth (i.e., the presence of specific male or female genitalia) and the secondary sex characteristics that develop later (facial and body hair, voice quality, etc.). Some are born as "hermaphrodites" wherein their primary sexual organs have features of both male and female organs making it extremely difficult to categorize the person as male or female. Another ambiguous sexual category consists of "transsexuals". Transsexuals are people who feel very strongly that the sexual organs they were born with do not conform to their deep-seated sense of what their sex should be.

Gender, on the other hand, refers to the culturally defined ways of acting as a male or a female that becomes part of an individual's personal sense of self. Gender socialization in a particular culture, religion, family, educational systems and others, tend to separate males and females into different social worlds with their own forms of activity and language. Edward Tylor, a 19th century British Anthropologist, had defined culture as "that complex whole which includes knowledge , belief, art, morals, law, custom and any other capabilities and habits acquired by man as a member of society".

As per sociological knowledge, all human societies are stratified by gender, meaning that males and females are channelised into specific statuses and roles. Status is the social position of a person in a society and role is the expected behavioural aspect or function of one's status. Until recently it was assumed that there were two separate spheres of life for men and women. Out of this gender-based division of labour emerged the notion of differences in a man and a woman's abilities and personalities. These differences were thought to be based on biological and psychological differences between man and woman. However, the 20th century social researchers had established and have evidence that gender roles are not innate or inborn but are strongly influenced by culture.

Education for Women's Equality and Empowerment

No nation, no society can progress towards desirable social change when half of its population is disabled. A march towards prosperity remains only an ideal, till the womenfolk actively participate in all the developmental activities. Education is seen as the one effective tool to empower women. "It is now widely held that modern education can mould people into enlightened, emphatic, risk-taking, thick skinned, industrious and mobile personalities. That education will be of immense help in bringing about democratization, secularism, national integration as well as economic prosperity and proper political socialization in the given country. It is generally believed by the people that axe of education can cut down the thick roots of traditions, superstitions, ignorance, backwardness, parochialism, etc" (Hemlata Talesra, 2004, p.87). Realizing the significance of education, the Indian Government has continuously stressed the importance of education and adopted measures to increase literacy amongst women. "In fact, education has been considered a vehicle to bring about a basic change in society and the status of women" (Rainuka Dagar (ed.) 1998, p.113). Education as an agency of desirable social change can empower women without visibly upsetting the age-old traditional ethos and sentiments, especially in a strong patriarchal society. As according to Rainuka Dagar, if empowerment means merely providing access, participation and skills within the existing gender differentiating system, it will remain a farce. Empowerment should mean an all round development and in this, education can play a crucial role in empowering women. According to Indira Gandhi, "Education is a liberating force, and in our age it is also a democratizing force, cutting across the barriers of caste and class, smoothing out inequalities imposed by birth and other circumstances". Also, like in the past, there is a strong connection between society and education.

The word education has its origin in the Latin word "educatum" composed of two terms 'E' and 'duco". "E" implies a progress from inward to outward while "duco" means developing or progressing. The dual terms, thus, would mean the process of developing the inner abilities and powers of an individual. The term is also related to the Latin word "educere", meaning 'to lead out' or 'to draw out', implying propulsion from the internal to the external. This term, educere, means to educate through a change brought about by practice or usage and implies some kind of change for the better in a person (Chandra, Soti Shivendra and Sharma, Rajendra K., 1996, p. 1).The term "education" can be sociologically understood in two ways. "In its broader sense education can mean any activity designed to impart knowledge and skills to enable a person to play an active role in society. In this sense education is nothing but socialization. Education in the stricter sense, also called formal education, is a conscious training to impart knowledge, values, skills and information in an institutionalized form over a stipulated period as a means to personality development as well as livelihood"(Alphonsus D'Souza., 2002, p. 38).

"Empowerment is an active, multi dimensional process which enables women to realize their full identity and powers in all sphere of life. Power is not a commodity to be transacted; nor can it be given away as alms. Power has to be sustained and preserved. Women have to empower themselves" (Jaya Kothai Pillai., 1995, preface). Discrimination of women from 'womb to tomb' is a well known fact, as such; empowerment through education can be an effective tool to change the status of women without visibly upsetting traditional strictures.

The Constitution of India, under Article 15 contains that there should be no "Prohibition of discrimination on grounds of religion, race, caste, sex or place of birth. It goes on to state further in Article 15(3), that nothing in this article shall prevent the state from making any special provision for women and children", and also Article 15(4) says that "Nothing in this article or in clause (2) of article 29 shall prevent the State from making any special provision for the advancement of any socially and educationally backward classes of citizens or for the scheduled castes and the scheduled tribes. Also, Article 41 gives the provision to 'Right to work, to education and to public assistance in certain cases'. Article 45 gives 'Provision for free and compulsory education for children (up to 14 years)'.Article 46 provides for the 'Promotion of educational and economic institute of scheduled castes, scheduled tribes and other weaker sections'. The State shall promote with special care the educational and economic interests of the weaker sections of the people, and in particular, of the scheduled castes and the scheduled tribes, and shall protect them from social injustice and all forms of exploitation'. Education, when backed in this manner by the constitution of India, can and will become an effective tool for empowerment of women.

The Education Commission (1964-66), realizing that change in knowledge, skills, interests and values of the people as a whole is necessary towards progressive change, has observed: "If this change on a grand scale is to be achieved without violent revolution (and then it would still be necessary) there is one instrument, and one instrument only that can be used, Education. Other agencies may help, and can indeed sometimes have a more apparent impression of greater impacts. But the ideal system of education is the only instrument that can be used to reach all levels of people, irrespective of gender, and empower them. "It is not, however, a magic wand to wave wishes into existence. It is a difficult instrument where effective use requires strength of will, 'dedicated' work and sacrifice. But it is a sure and tried instrument, which has served other countries well in their struggle for development. It can, given the will and the skill, do so for India" (Agrawal, S. P and Agrawal, J. C, 1991, p. 109 – 110). Equality of opportunity when curbed cannot promote desirable social change.

Comparative Sketch of Two Societies and an Individual Woman from the Past

Angami Nagas, Nagaland: Education came to the Angami area through the Christian missionaries who promoted literacy so that the new Christian converts could read the Bible and sing hymns. The Government also did not lag behind but established its own schools and even supported the missionary schools. As a result, almost all Angami villages have at least one Government school, and one or more private schools run by the Christian churches. But higher education was not available till the 1940s when some high schools were established. But it may be noted that though there was equal enthusiasm shown by both the genders, the male members got better privileges and preference as compared to the girls even in the early days

- a pure case of making way for the manfolks because culture says so. College education came to the Angami area only when Kohima Science College was established in 1961 and the Kohima College in 1967. However, in recent years there has been an extraordinary growth in the number of schools and colleges, the latter receiving a boost after the establishment of Nagaland University in 1992. Kohima District, according to 2001 Census, has 74.28% literacy rate with 81.40% for males and 66.54% for females. According to Aphuno Chase Roy, to the Angamis, "Education gave a sense of achievement; an upward mobility and modern lifestyle . . .". Thus in the Angami area education at all levels is accessible to almost all. Yet, patriarchy is so strong that the status of women has not made too many changes in spite of modern education, even in literate urban areas too.

Kalpeni Islanders, Lakshadweep: The Kalpeni Islanders are basically Muslims who follow the pattern of Islamic faith with a difference. They also practice a special type of matriliny. In the matriarchal Kalpeni society, female links alone are recognized for the sharing and transmission of the exogamous matrilineal descent group known as the "taravad". A taravad is a group of individuals, comprising of both males and females who traces their descent line from the female line from a single female ancestor.

The traditional pattern for residence, after marriage is duo local and at times is referred to as "visiting marriage". Even after marriage, the spouses would continue to live in their own taravads, with the husband spending nights at his wife's residence and returning to his own taravad in the morning. The children become members of the mother's taravad. There were very rare instances of the usual conjugal family of husband, wife and children.

The menfolks of the Kalpeni Islanders are not, however, helpless. An elderly man from a taravad, who is also called the Karnavar, becomes the manager of properties, organize production, and assign work to younger male members of the groups. The Karnavars, up to this day have to be under the authority of their matriarch.

According to the 2001 census, Lakshadweep Island's literacy rate was a high 87.52%. The male literacy rate being 93.15% and the female being 81.56%. However, not too conspicuous changes have been observed even in this very strong matriarchal society.

Case Study of Mevuhole Koso, Daughter of Pucho Koso and Kropale

Mevuhole was the daughter of a very rich man in Viswema. She has a sister known by the name Neizehole. The sisters were without male siblings in a patrilineal Angami Naga society. When the sisters came of age, they were married to two influential men in their own village. Since their father was a man of high social standing there was no discrimination or ill-treatment to the two sisters. Their father, however, while on his way to Khonoma village to buy necklaces for his daughters tripped, fell and died of his injuries, later, at his own village. The two sisters grew up normally, got married and bore children. The younger sister gave birth to a girl and a boy and fitted comfortably into the society.

The elder sister, Mevuhole's case was different. She married a handsome and respectable young man named Vikhwel Vitsu from her village. He was wealthy according to the village standard of those days i.e. before the World War II. He enjoyed honour and prestige in the village because of his philanthropic ways which were attributes of his wealth and his humane heart. He and his wife Mevuhole also gave feast of merit for five times to their villagers which was considered to be feat only the rich could afford. Feast of Merit involved the use of huge quantity of rice, fire-wood and many cows. The large demographic composition of Viswema village poses a greater challenge as it is the second largest village amongst the Angami tribe, the third largest village in Nagaland and also the third largest village in Asia. Apparently, a man has to be wealthy to perform such feats to earn special status in the society. Every feast of merit is followed by stone-pulling. Stone-pulling ceremony is a process where the whole village comes together in their traditional fineries, feasts together and pulls stone monoliths from far-off jungles to commemorate the 'Feast of Merit'. He and his wife owned the biggest log drum in Viswema village where Zutho (local rice beer) was brewed in large quantities and served during festivals and ceremonial feasts. They also had the privilege to live in a wooden-roofed house which only a few owned in their village. The tragedy was that he died young leaving his wife with two daughters in a society where family without male issues was considered to be an incomplete family.

Fig.1: Mevuhole's monoliths at John High School, Viswema

As a widow, Mevuhole tried her best to bring up her two daughters like a normal family. She owned many plots of forests and terraced fields in prime locations. These landed properties were from her inheritance, her deceased husband's agnatic properties and the bulk of it from acquired landed property. She also bought water rights from people who live above her fields by slaughtering some of her cows and giving portions to them in exchange for the right to control the water that flows down from the village to her fields. This ensured adequate water for irrigating her fields. She cultivated fields equivalent to three-four average families put together. This was possible because of hiring seasonal labourers during transplanting and harvesting seasons of the life cycle of the paddy. Many families also borrowed paddy from her in lean seasons and worked for her as repayment when she needed additional manpower. However, many vied to work in her fields, especially in summer, because of her generosity and her reputation of providing fats of pork preserved from the previous winter. This was another status symbol basically because only a rich person can afford to have a huge *Ovo Lahe. Ovo Lahe,* in Viswema dialect, is referred to the long, big slices of fats acquired from big pigs slaughtered during *Sekrenyi* (the chief festival of the Angamis) and preserved by hanging inside the house. It has a peculiar taste which is relished and, therefore, given to special people. The length and breadth of which is also a matter of envy and the centre of many a conversation in Angami homes.

Land could be easily acquired in those days if one had wealth because needs of varied nature arise like every other society which also ensured the transfer of properties from one person to the next. Among the animists, when a person dies, cows are slaughtered and distributed to all who attend the funeral house. This practice has religious implications as well as social implications. It has social relevance because people who cannot afford a cow on their deaths were looked down by the society. This need, as well as the need for consumption, made the cow a necessary animal and naturally those who own many numbers of cows are at an advantage to gain wealth. Again, a person has to have paddy because cowboys were paid in kind. As a widow, Mevuhole owned many cows and also acquired huge landed properties in this manner too. She was much richer than when she was with her husband. She was very industrious too. She and her daughters had lots of paddy and many cows which were important determinants of wealth in the traditional Angami society.

After her husband's death; Mevuhole desired higher status for herself and her daughters. This ambition stemmed from the fact that after her husband's death, she could not earn the prestigious thigh of cows which is given to persons who have performed 'feast of merit' twice or more. She was entitled to a slice of meat only from every performer hosting the feast of merit as a widow. It was not necessarily the need for bigger shares of meat for consumption but the prestige and honour that followed when one is qualified to receive the prestigious thigh of cows from new entrants to earn positions of higher status in the village. This position is earned purely by merit unlike ascribed status. Thus, Mevuhole decided to earn the feast of merit in order to be at par with her husband's contemporaries in spite of his early death which is followed by stone pulling.

Her two stone monoliths still stands at John High School, Viswema, a School founded and named after her elder son-in-law who was illiterate but was a pioneer of modern education in the Angami society. A widow was rarely found to go to that extent in those days because it involved a lot of wealth. She enjoyed honour, prestige and high social standing because of her achievements and wealth.

However, her wealth turned out to be her greatest enemy when her daughters were approaching marriageable age, because she did not have a male heir. She had married off her elder daughter before the war and when her younger daughter was also approaching marriageable age, after Word War II, one of her husband's nephews came early one morning with a cock and a spear to occupy their house forcibly. Customarily, it was considered to be unlawful to chase out a widow and her children in order to forcefully claim inheritance of the house and agnatic properties of her husband during their lifetime. Not all widows get treated like this because there is a belief and an unspoken fear that evil things befall upon those who treat the living as dead. Therefore, it was considered to be a taboo to behave in that manner. But this did not deter the errant nephew to forego his claims. When the clan members of Mevuhole's husband came to know about the incident, they gathered and collectively chased away the nephew, warning of dire consequences in case of repetition. Thereafter, she lived peacefully at her marital house, married off her younger daughter and went about her normal life. When she was getting too old, out of her own volition, she decided to vacate her house to her errant husband's nephew. Thus, Mevuhole bought her own plot of land, near her elder daughter's house, and built her own house. She gifted her house to one of her grandsons. She lived to a ripe old age and died.

Fig.2: Epitaph of Mevuhole at Viswema daughters. These were gifted from acquired properties

The saga of Mevuhole did not end with her death because her younger daughter also had four daughters without male siblings. The younger daughter of Mevuhole had married a respectable man but he died before reaching his prime old age, leaving his widow with four daughters and an adopted son. Adoption was allowed by performing certain ceremonies, proclamation and observation of a one day Genna by all clan members. Life was normal for Mevuhole's younger daughter even after her husband's death. She continued the formal education of her younger daughters and adopted son even after the dead of her husband. She married off her daughters to educated men and got grandsons and grand-daughters from all her daughters. She also gave forests land and terraced-fields to each of her also her share of property that she had inherited from her parents, mostly from her mother Mevuhole. Her daughters also all pursued higher education and are presently engaged as working mothers and are earning their own livelihood in their marital homes with their husbands.

Conclusion

Against the backdrop given, a few issues may be raised and deliberated. Mevuhole, a formal uneducated woman could achieve a very high status for herself, wield power, acquire immense wealth, gave two feast of merit as a widow and could leave property for her daughters to inherit is a feat that cannot be imagined now in the 21st Century. The Angami society is also considered to be one of the strongest patriarchal societies in the Naga society and the village in question, Viswema, is the second largest village in Angami land. As such, Mevuhole is a self-made woman who could raise her status to a very high level because of her hard-working nature, good decision-making strategies, good relations especially with her husband's clan members and the ability to influence others. She was a great moralist and a strict disciplinarian who advocated humility that earned respect. Thus, in the past, even for women, it was quite possible for those who were willing to raise their status by striving towards it rather than demanding it from others.

The Naga society as a whole has been on a war-footing to spread formal education both in the rural and urban areas. Many are getting educated but the "education that truly liberates and empowers is sadly lacking in both men and women". For men, the ethos of the patriarchal set-up helps them to some extent but for women; the present educational system had worsened their situation as far as their status is concerned except for a handful of ladies who have been empowered through better educational institutions which imparted quality education. The same goes for the Kalpeni Islanders, who with 81.56% female literacy rate, still have very low status for its women folks which also shows that high literacy rate is not going to be the answer for uplifting the status of women. Educational system needs to be examined and the educated needs should be observed to see the viability of the formal education that is imparted to our people, especially to women. An education that truly empowers without making demands to be recognized needs to become the basis of education. This will help save on time, money and energy to be used ethically and purposefully.

The question of: Whether education can lead to upward social mobility and liberate conservative thinking? Whether education should be viewed as a worthwhile investment, as some thinks on the lines of "human capital theory", especially on the girl child education? Whether education can play a pivotal role in bringing about a balanced gender equation in all spheres of life? While examining these issues, one must keep in mind that the literacy rate is accounted, according to the Census of India, for all persons who can read and write with understanding in any language. This includes children of 7 years and above too. Therefore, the literacy rate can be a misleading factor at times.

In Nagaland, according to 2001 Census, the literacy rate is 67.11% overall. The literacy rate for males being 71.70% and females being 61.92%. Therefore, it is not too low as compared to other States in India but, useable, confident and efficient manpower, is an outcome of education that truly empowers which is still lacking in both the genders. This makes us to compare the educational system emphasized in other developed countries, like the United States where children become independent by the age of 18 years and moves out of parents homes even. In our Naga context this is not at all practical until the children are secured with a job or until they get married. All this are indications that our educational system is not empowering us as it is supposed to. Another deliberation can be, whether the right teaching methods are used by persons who are capable of imparting qualitative education? Whether parents and the whole societal set-up is playing a complimentary role to achieve the true educational goals? Whether our schools and colleges are just trying to get the best statistical result percentage? We must examine and see if there is any defect in the syllabus provided by the Universities or whether it has become obsolete in this 21st Century? Is the prevalent educational system only suitable for gearing up our youngsters towards government jobs and not even entrepreneurial avenues where proficiency is a required quality? There must be some lapses and gaps between societal needs and the educational system. For instance, the educational qualification a person gets is based on bookish knowledge. The spoon feeding system used by the teachers due to the pressures of the result oriented examination system and the memorizing culture frequently adopted by students may be the main hurdles to quality education.

The Naga society is undergoing a process of social change towards modernization. Towards this change, education is the most effective tool to equip us to move on to a desirable social change. But if, neither in a patriarchal or a matriarchal society, education is not empowering, then the educational system with all its related organizations and institutions needs to be evaluated and loopholes need to be rectified. In a strong Patriarchal Naga society, the only way to bring about a silent revolution in order to raise the status of women is to give the right educational input; an education which will really and truly give an all round development. It is also a fact that Naga women are not entirely stagnated with the traditional status set aside for women but they are sandwiched in between the traditional and the modern statuses. The modern status is based on achieved status, using education as the main source of status propulsion. A sizeable percentage of Naga men and women have excelled themselves in quality education and have also being able to raise their status to impressive heights on, almost, equal bars. Thus, on a positive note, gender studies on education, is not a negative competition for the male and female to outdo, dominate or suppress each other but is in fact a struggle to make both genders to become wholesome in order to compliment each other towards healthy societal growth. In fact, it should never be linked with extreme feminist theories but must be studied neutrally for the sake of wholesome development for the society as a whole. Women comprise of half of the population in almost every society and so when this portion of the society is disabled it surely hampers the growth of the society. A limping man can never outrun a person whose legs are both fit and balanced, so also both the genders needs to be empowered to move on to desirable social change. And it is only common sense that we give special emphasis to the weaker leg, strengthen it and empower it so as to run efficiently towards desired goals.

REFERENCES

1. Agrawal, J.C; 1993; *Landmarks in the History of Modern Education;* New Delhi; Vikash Publishing House (P) Ltd.
2. Agrawal, S.P & J.C. Agrawal; 1991; *Educational and Social Uplift of Backward Classes-Part 1;* New Delhi; Concept Publishing Company.
3. Basu, Durga Das; 2004; *Shorter Constitution of India (13th Edition);* New Delhi; Wadhwa and Company Law Publishers.
4. Chandra, Soti Shivendra & Rajendra K. Sharma; 1996; *Principles of Education;* New Delhi; Atlantic Publishers and Distributors.
5. Dagar, Rainuka (ed.); 1998; *Manual on Women's Development and Gender Justice;* Chandigarh; Institute for Development and Communication (IDC).
6. Downs, Frederick S; 1992; 'North East India in the Nineteenth and Twentieth Centuries' in *History of Christianity in India,* Vol. V, Part 5; Bangalore; Church History Association of India.
7. D'Souza, Alphonsus & Kekhrieseno Christina; 2002; *Coping with Social Change in North-East India: A Comparative Study of Three Ethnic Groups in North-East India (Aka, Angami and Dimasa);* St. Joseph's College, Jakhama, Nagaland.
8. Ghosh, B.B; 'Problems of Writing the History of Nagaland' in J. B. Bhattacharjee (ed.) *Studies in the History of Nagaland;* Shillong; NEHU Publications.
9. Gore, M.S; 1994; *Indian Education: Structure and Process;* New Delhi; Rawat Publications.
10. Liegise, Buno; 2006; *The Struggle of Rural Women and Winds of Change in Nagaland;* Hudi Dielie, Angami Students Union, Issue No. I.
11. Pillai, Jaya Kothai; 1995; *Women and Empowerment;* New Delhi; Gyan Publishing House.
12. Rege, Sharmila; 2003; *Sociology of Gender;* New Delhi; Sage Publications.
13. Roy, Aphuno Chase; 2004; *Women in Transition: Angami Naga Women from 1878 to the Present;* (Published by the Author).
14. Talesra, Hemlata; 2004; *Sociological Foundations of Education;* New Delhi; Kanishka Publishers & Distributors.
15. Ulich, Robert; *History of Educational Thought;* New Delhi; Eurasia Publishing House (P) Ltd.

16. Zehol, Lucy; 1998; *Women in Naga Society*; New Delhi; Regency Publications.

17. Directorate of Economics & Statistics; *Statistical Hand Book of Nagaland – 2006;* Government of Nagaland.

18. Indira Gandhi National Open University; 1990; *ESO-02: Women and Society;* New Delhi.

19. Indira Gandhi National Open University; 1990; *ESO-02: Women and Society;* New Delhi.

7

Status of Women with Special Reference to Naga Society

Athungo Ovung

"Custom is to society what Law is to State"

- *Salmond*

Introduction

The word 'status' has various meanings and is used in different ways. In sociological literature it is often used as a synonym for role. Diametrically opposite views have been expressed, while a few writers have referred to the legal rights enjoyed by women in marriage, inheritance and participation in public affairs, while others have referred to the still prevalent inequality and discrimination suffered by women due to the social attitudes of males and the existing customs and traditions. As *Malinowski* has pointed out, correct definitions of status can be given only after taking into consideration all mutual duties between the sexes against the high-handedness of the other. *Lowie* has shown that status may mean four different things, all four of which may not be, however, found to co-exist anywhere. Thus, actual treatment, legal status opportunity for social participation and the character and extent of work, all determine each in a specific sense and manner, the status of women in a society. All these four determinants are independent of each other and not causally related. The correlation between them is empirical and not conceptual.

Functionalists maintain sex differentiation contributes to overall social stability, but conflict theorist charges that the relationship between females and males is one of unequal power, with men dominating women. This dominance shows up in people's everyday interactions. Feminism as an ideology has developed as a consequence of historical process. Feminism can be considered as; a) A holistic theory concerned with the nature of women's global oppression and subordination to men; b) A social-political theory and practice which aims to free all women from female supremacy and exploitation; c) A social movement encompassing strategic confrontation with the sex-class system; and d) An ideology, which stands in dialectical opposition to all misogynous ideologies and practices (Jary & Jary, 2000, p, 211)

The Feminist movement of the United States born in upstate New York, in a town called Seneca Falls, in the summer of 1848. The first wave of Feminist fought for legal and political equality for women. They were not afraid to risk controversy on behalf of their cause, in 1872; Susan B. Antony was arrested for attempting to vote in that year's presidential election (Richard T. Schaeffer, 2006, p, 284). The 'second wave' of feminist is concerned with understanding and documenting an oppression believed to be commonly experienced by all women and further emphasized the diversity of women's relationships not only to the male social order but also to each other. The original four demands of the 'second wave' were equal pay, equal education and opportunities free contraception, abortion on demand and free 24-hour miseries have been identified as the primary concern of white western women. Access to food, fuel and water are the primary needs of many third world women, including tribal women (Jary & Jary, 2000, p, 211).

The commission as the status on women (CSW) is one of the first body established by the UN Economics and Social Council, set up in 1946, it monitors the situation of women and promotes their rights to all societies around the world. It prepares and recommends and reports for the UN on any issue effecting women. In case of urgent problems, the commission can press for imitate international action to prevent or alleviate violation of women rights. The needs for integrating women in the development process were placed on the international agenda in 1975, when the UN observed International Women Year. Among the many concrete steps taken after the 1975 World Conference on women was the formation of the two UN bodies, UNIFEN and INSTRAN.

In the national context, constitutional and legal safeguards are provided to ameliorate the status of women. Some of the safeguarding issues are as follows;

Constitutional safeguards are: a) Article 14- Equality before law, b) Article 15- No discrimination on the basis of sex, caste etc, c) Article16-Equality of opportunity, d) Article 19- Six Fundamental Freedom (Speech and expression, assembly, association, movement, residence and settlement and occupation). e) Article 21- Right to life and personal property. f) Article 23- Prohibits trafficking. g) Article 39-47-Means of livelihood, equal pay, protection of health, maternity relief, etc.

Legal Safeguards

Some of the important sections of Indian Penal Code (IPC) protecting and upholding status of women are as follows:

Section 302/304B	-	Deals with punishment for homicide for dowry, dowry deaths or the attempts
Section 354	-	Outrage of women's modesty
Section 363-373	-	Kidnapping and abduction.
Section 366A and 366B	-	Procurator and importation of girl to force or seduce illicit intercourse with another person
Section 376	-	Relating to rape
Section 498A	-	Enticement of women to illicit intercourse with another person
Section 509	-	Insulting the modesty of women.

The status of women varies from society to society, culture to culture, region to region, and tribe to tribe. In Indian society and *Naga* society particularly such diversity in the status of women are quite evident. The *Nagas* culture, since the very early periods, women as a group has been dominated by men and their status has been low in the family and society. However, status of tribal women is far better than plainsmen in certain aspects, e.g., absence of dowry, presence of bride-price, Sati, status of widow, etc. but there are also certain aspects where they are left behind, such as relating to right to inheritance, political participation and so on. In the relationship between men and women, it is the fact that men are stronger than women so far as physical strength is concerned. But then there are other areas like IQ, patience, tolerance, education, technical experiences where women can compete and succeed.

Unlike other Hindu societies, the *Nagas* have their own customary laws which is linked to their indigenous issue. These tribes present them as a mechanism essential to safeguard their identity that has been observed right from the early days (history). Women in these regions were denied of participation in decision-making, mode of inheritance, adoption, occupational choice and so on. Traditional beliefs and practices are often the root cause of gender gap, keeping girls at home to supplement family welfare, sometimes income. Often, families in remote villages feel they have no choice but to discontinue sending their daughters to school as there are no alternative opportunities to supplement house hold income and welfare. However, financial problem is not only the factor for illiteracy in most of our villages but ignorance on the part of both the parents and sometimes, obstinate children. There is an old saying that an intelligent has an intelligent mother and studies to reveal that girls with literate mothers are more likely to go to school than girls with illiterate mothers (*Nagaland Post*, Dated: 03/06/07).

Nagaland

Nagas are the Mongoloid Tribe inhabiting the hilly region between the river of Brahmaputra and Chindwin river of Myanmar. It is bounded by Myanmar in the east, Assam in the west,

Arunachal Pradesh and part of Assam in the north and Manipur in the south. There are eleven districts and fifteen tribes speaking more than fifty languages and dialects. The population of Nagaland is almost entirely tribal. Originally, all the *Naga* tribes had their own separate identity and they were known by their own tribes in their respective dialects, custom and culture.

The position of women in the *Naga* communities is comparatively high when compared with the rest of the country. They are honoured for their role in the family. Majority of the domestic affairs are in the hands of the women. She is an example as well as a teacher of hard work for her children. It is the duty of women to nurture her children. The mother is to look after and take care of her children which may be said as a bounding duty. The society, therefore, respects her as a 'mother' and this may be called the status of female in a respectable sense. Today with the fast changing world, we find that the status of women is gaining a higher position where she can enjoy her right almost equally with that of a man in every aspect of life. In the N*aga* society, we find that the present women are educated and equipped with office works, trade and commerce, business administrations etc., which in turn brings higher economic input in the family as well as for the society as a whole. One cannot deny the fact that with each passing year women are showing higher degree of performance. Women have achieved parity with men in obtaining college degrees and are employed in top professions today. The Naga women are in no way inferior to men in the contemporary stage, though a man plays the lead role in every aspect of life in their society.

The Nagas have their customary laws and courts from time immemorial. However, there are certain areas where women are left behind. Women were not given the right to inheritance especially immovable property, to take part in decision-making body, to initiate divorce, guardianship and adoption, custody of children, choice of life partner, occupation and so on. Thus, we see that customary laws are based on inequality between men and women. Traditional values and practices still treat women as inferiors. This notion has so long chained them that it still hinders them from full and active participation in today's social system. Even educated women are reluctant to be seen as 'women libber' or 'feminists'. The greatest barriers against emancipation of women are the traditional values and practices, which needs special action.

Women in the Family

The traditional *Naga* family is nuclear and exogamous which is both patriarchal and patrilineal in nature. The father is the supreme authority of the family. Sometimes the father exercises his power and authority in consultation with his wife and the grown up children. As head of the family, he is responsible for the maintenance and protection of the whole family. He is the sole decision maker with regard to every matter that arises within the family's circle. The father represents the family on any public gathering or any matter related to the public service. All the earnings of the individual members of the family go to the common fund of the family under the control of the father. He takes a leading part in the marriage of his sons and daughters, and performs his religious duties during important festivals and other important occasions or ceremonies. The father of the family portions out his lands and other properties amongst his children and makes necessary provisions for his wife in the event of his death. He represents his family in the clan meetings and at the village court.

A wife generally helps her husband in the discharge of his duties especially in the management of household affairs. The wife is also consulted in all important matters relating to the family affairs. The mother is solely responsible for cooking of food, fetching drinking water, collection of fire woods, collection of vegetables, spinning and weaving, cooking and washing, sowing seeds and vegetables, feeding of children and domestic animals, delivery attendant, house cleaning, fetching water, barter of vegetables, Gardening, embroidery works, preparation of yeast, distillation of country liquor, and so on. In the event of unfortunate disablement of the husband, the wife is to shoulder all the responsibilities of her husband in the maintenance of the family. This is also equally applicable in case of widow mother. So long the children specially the sons are not grown up and eligible to assist their mother in the maintenance of the family. The widow lives as a member of the family along with her children until she marries or survives. She has ever right to enjoy her husband's property for her livelihood but she loses her rights and authority once she remarries.

Women in Decision-making

The unwritten customs, cultural patterns, conventions, social norms and values had been established by old-age usages and practices by the member of the *Naga* society. As far as the Naga customary law is concerned women have no place in decision-making whether within the family or outside the family. The decision on the administration of the village and the society exclusively rest with men. Women were ignored in most of the important functions. They were not given rights to represent any clan, village decision matter. Though, the tribal woman dominates in socio-economic activities, their participation in the political processes and governance is practically nil. The village council which are elected bodies does not have even a single woman representative from the state. No woman has ever become the head or chief of the village. Thus in the traditional system women are debarred from the decision-making body of the society.

Status in Terms of Inheritance

The Nagas are a patrilocal and patrilineal people. They trace their descent through the male members and their properties pass from the father to his son. Man inherits the entire parental properties. In fact, women have no say in this matter unless and until the head of the family gives it as a 'gift' or 'will'. A woman, either a wife or a daughter, is not considered in the matter of succession to the headship. They do not have any legal claim on the family property. A widow with minor son cannot sell or dispose off their property. In the absence of a male child, the nearest male relative becomes the legal head. A son can inherit the property of a family be it ancestral or self-acquired property of his father. The daughters in a family are usually excluded from the inheritance list, but in some cases like a sonless family or abundant self-acquired properties, they may be offered with some part of the properties. The daughters, before their marriage, could enjoy the properties of the family. But, as soon as they are married, such privileges cease to exist.

The daughters can inherit some of the materials which are partly in the nature of their personal belongings like, weaving materials and ornaments of their mother in addition to some clothes in the form of presentations at the time of marriage. The women folk are generally excluded from inheritance of any property, but they can enjoy the property as long as they remain within the circle of the family. A woman can purchase properties by using the money given by her parents yet; her own sons only can inherit those properties. In no case or condition, these properties can be diverted back to her parents or their family members. The unmarried sons and daughters enjoy the same privileges at their parents' home with whatever wealth the family possesses.

On the event of the death of the husband, the widow retains the house and all other properties for rearing and maintaining her children. The widow can retain the property as long as she is alive and does not marry another person. But, if the widow remarries, then from that very moment, she will have to surrender all claims over the properties of her former husband and leave for her present husband's home with the only clothes she wears.

Status in Terms of Marriage and Divorce

There are different forms, rituals and conditionality of marriage which are found among the Nagas. It varies from tribe to tribe and even within the same tribe. Though, there are different forms of marriage prevalent among the Nagas such as monogamy, polygamy, exogamy and so on, there are some similarities as by nature Nagas are patriarchal and patrilineal. The Nagas practice bride price which is almost present in all the society. But, this should not be mistaken that she is not purchased as in the case of dowry system, where the bride has to pay the groom. There are some materials that are to be given to the bride's family by the bridegroom, such as dao, sickle, salt, basket, *hanlamso,* etc. Marriage between blood-related members is not allowed under any circumstance.

Women have a very low position in choice of life partners. Everything is arranged by their parents especially the head of the family. She has no right to receive any property of her parents except some dresses and ornaments from her mother. After marriage a women has no right to interfere in her parent's affairs. She is completely cut out from the family property and surrenders to her husband. Divorce is common among the Nagas, where fines are imposed if the divorce is not made on reasonable grounds. In respect of divorce there is hardly a case where a woman initiates divorce. When couples divorce, only the husband is entitled to the custody of the children. A mother cannot claim her children after divorce. If maintenance of children is granted to the wife, she will continue to do so at the infancy stages of the child. But, there is no limit as for how long she can continue to do so. Women are always looked down in the matter of elopement, divorce and remarriage. A wife who is divorced on grounds of sexual immorality or of defamation of the husband and his family, however, is not entitled to receive any maintenance of property though she can look after her infant child for sometime after which, the child has to go back to the father. A woman has no right to claim children after divorce by all means.

Status in Terms of Guardianship, Custody of Children and Maintenance

Nagas who are patriarchal in nature, the father is the absolute guardian of the family as long as he lives. Women have no right to claim guardianship, custody of children and maintenance except for a short period of time to look and take care of the children. When the natural guardians die, the eldest son in the family customarily becomes the next guardian. Even if the natural guardians die leaving an infant child, the mother has no authority in decision making even if she acts as the guardian. The mother can act as the guardian only if she does not marry again. For decision-making, she depends on her in-laws for all necessary issues until the child attains the age to look after the family affairs.

Maintenance takes place when the couple are divorced or separated. A widow can maintain the family's property such as; house, lands and fields etc., as long as she remains in the family. She can do so even in the case of separate residence if she chooses to remain single. But, it entirely depends on the husband's family whether she should be given any maintenance. If maintenance of children is granted to the wife, then she continues to do so at the infancy stages of the child, but once she gets married it stops.

Remedies

- Customary laws have to be change and evolve. The society women in particular should counter its laws that exclude woman from the right to property inheritance, participation in decision making bodies and equality within the family *and* change them in favour of equality.
- Economic empowerment should be given to the women such as ownership of assets (movable or immovable) to enhance their sense of self-confidence.
- Empowering women through education should be given prior importance.
- Initiative should be taken right from the grass root (rural areas) level through various organizations, agencies including non governmental organization by organizing campaign, seminar and so on.

REFERENCES

1. Ahlawat, Neerja; 1995; *Women Organisation and Social Networks;* Jaipur; Rawat Publications.
2. Biju, M.R; 2006; *Women's Empowerment;* New Delhi; Mittal Publications.
3. Hutton, J.H; 1921; *The Angami Naga*; London; Oxford University Press.

4. Jain, S.P & Mamata Singh; 2001; *Violence against Women;* New Delhi; Radha Publications.

5. Jary, D & Jary; 2000; *Sociology;* Glasgow; Harper Collins Publishers.

6. Joseph, S. Thong; 1997; *Head-Hunters Culture (Historic Culture of Nagas);* Kohima; Nei-u Printing Press.

7. Mills, J.P; 1922; *The Lotha Nagas;* London; Oxford University Press.

8. Plamer, P; 1989; *Contemporary Women's Fiction;* London; Harvest.

9. Ramegowda, A; 1997; *Gender Inequality: Power Privilege and Poverty in Plantations;* Jaipur; Rawat Publications.

10. Vyas, Anju & Sunita Singh; 1993; *Women's Studies in India: Information Sources, Services and Programmes;* New Delhi; Sage Publications.

11. Government of Nagaland; Directorate of Economics & Statistics; *Statistical Handbook of Nagaland - 2001;* Kohima.

12. *Nagaland Post;* Dated-Dimapur, 03.06.07

8

Inheritance and Gender Implications with Special Reference to the Southern Angami Group

Christina Kekhrieseno

The traditional habitat of the Angami corresponds more or less to the central and southern parts of Kohima district and part of Dimapur. The area is mountainous, with very high peaks and elevated ridges, irregular spurs and deep valleys. *Japfü*, the second highest peak in Nagaland is situated almost in the centre of the Angami area.

The *Gazetteer of Kohima* describes the Angami country in the following words; "summits of the lofty peaks are thickly wooded, clad with evergreen vegetation; they abound in varied flora and fauna. The lower hills have become deforested owing to the practice of both slash and burn and terrace cultivation." (Gazetteer 1970:2).

The Southern Angamis is also known as *Zuonuo-Keyhonuo*. They also prefer to call themselves as *Japfüphiki* meaning those living in the vicinity of *Japfü* peak. In any case, the *Zuonuo-Keyhonuo* group continues to remain part of the Angami, though it forms structurally and culturally, a distinct socio-territorial group (Bareh 2001:159). The area is a compact geographical unit covering 403.8 sq. km, the National Highway passes through

Kohima going towards Manipur and traverses the entire southern Angami area. It links the most important villages of *Pheṣama, Kigwema, Jakhama, Viswema* and *Khuzama*. It also provides an access to other villages situated away from the Highway. A road from Mao traversing along the ridge of the *Kedi-Kezo-Chazuo range link Kedima, Kezoma and Kezobasa to Chakhabama* (D,Souza 2001: 36-37). Godwin Austen in 1872 describes this region as "no part of the Barrial is more beautiful than that between Kigwema and Sopvomah, looking up the lateral glacial gorges with their frowning, steep sides, running up to the crest of the Barrial, which is for the greater part made up of a wall gray of rocks and precipice. Dense forest covers the slopes breaking the usual monotony of the dark-coloured mountain scenery. Where the steep rise in the slope commences, the spurs are at once more level, and are terraced for rice cultivation; not a square yard of available land has been left and the system of irrigation canals is well laid out. I have never, even in the better -cultivated parts of the Himalayas, seen terrace cultivation carried to such perfection, and it gives a peculiarly civilized appearance to the country (quoted in Elwin 1969:578-588).

Status of Women

The term 'status' refers to position and thus the term 'status of women' refers to the position of women in a given society along with the rights and duties attached to the position. Usually, the status of women is measured and identified in opposition to the status of men. Men are 'bread winners' and women are 'home makers' is the usual norm. However, such a division is not biological in origin but socially created. Hence, sociologists make a distinction between sex and gender. The word 'sex' is used to refer to biological attributes of men and women and the word 'gender' to the distinctive qualities of men and women that are culturally created (Epstein 1988). Therefore, gender based division is discriminatory of women. Women are considered inferior, their work as less important and so men are the 'bread winners' and custodians of property while women are good for home and care of children, thus, strengthening patriarchy and male dominance.

There is a general view that tribal women especially in the North East are more privileged than others in terms of freedom and decision making as compared to their counterparts in the mainland India. Haimendorf expressed the same view when he said, "many women in most civilized parts of India may well envy the women of the Naga Hills their high status and happy life; and if you measure the cultural level of a people by the social position and personal freedom of its women, you will think twice before looking down on the Nagas as "savages" (Haimendorf 1939:101). Similar view was also expressed by Hutton.

Traditionally Angami women enjoyed a fairly high status because traditionally women played an important role in the domestic sphere as well as in the economic activities. The economic contribution of tribal women is greater than that of women in caste society (Pathy 1988: 179-182). Shifting cultivation is sometimes described as "female cultivation" (Deeney and Fernandes 1992:62) not only because women put in more work but chiefly because major decisions concerning cultivation are taken by women. Similarly the terrace cultivation among the Angami Nagas has been described as 'female farming' (D'Souza 2001:52).

The most striking difference between the Angami and other Naga tribes is the practice of terrace cultivation and wet fields while other tribes practice shifting cultivation (Hutton1969: 72). *Jhum* cultivation is also practiced to some extent. However, Angami economy has been changing ever since the colonial administration set foot in the area (Sema 1992: 93-138). Thus, the Angami area is also experiencing the consequences of social processes like globalization, urbanization, population growth and changing land relations which actually affect women's control over their livelihood. This as mentioned earlier, is because women cultivators have a better position when engaged in cultivation since they take major decision with agricultural activities. Today, land is treated as a commodity easily bought and sold. This commodification of land has adversely affected the economic independence of women. Non-agricultural occupations are becoming the mainstay of the economy. No doubt educated women are on the rise and they are also being employed in the tertiary sector but this does not ensure them a higher status for they are expected to share family burden.

Property and Inheritance

The Angami Nagas are patrilineal and patriarchal. Hence, men exercise authority and inheritance along the male line. There are differences in the pattern of inheritance between the Western, Northern and Southern Angami, but such differences need not be over emphasized.

Property is a socially sanctioned recognition of a group or individual's rights, privileges, and responsibilities with relation to an object, resource or activity (Scott 199:318). Therefore, property refers to those relationships that exist between people and things along with the sets of rights attached to the things.

The concept of individual ownerships implies the idea of exclusive, though total exclusiveness is probably not possible in a tribal society. Among the Angamis, the practice of individual ownership is well established but there are also certain residual rights preserved by the community such as collecting dry twigs for firewood or green edible from some one's forest is not restricted. Communal ownership is vested in clan, families, village and even tribe. Individual property is either acquired or inherited through well established norms of inheritance.

According to normal customary laws, women do not inherit ancestral landed property but they can use them even for a life time. However, they can inherit acquired property of their parents. Hence, customarily women are at a disadvantage. In India laws relating to property rights are generally discriminatory of women. 'Customary laws deriving from religion or other sources, as also enacted laws do not give women the same rights as men (Sivaramayya 1991; Saxena 1991). Among the *Zuonuo-Keyhonuo* group, there is a possibility for a woman to inherit even ancestral property, for instance, in the case of issueless man, his daughter can occupy the parental house but, the patrilineal system requires that a symbolic transfer of a small piece of land to the nearest male kin to ensure the transfer of ancestral property *(Kayie)* in the male line. Thus, tribal customary laws are patriarchal in nature.

Traditionally, a woman has rights only over her personal property like clothes, ornaments, baskets and weaving kit. When she marries she may be gifted with paddy and terrace field acquired by the parents. She may even get terrace field from her mother. This is a special feature practice among the *Zuonuo-Keyhonuo*. But, such a privilege is enjoyed only when her mother owns a field. It is also to be noted that in a family of many daughters, all do not get to inherit such landed property.

As a wife, she inherits certain rights over her husband's property, manages them, cultivates, gathers, stores and distributes them. In the agricultural set-up, she controls the agricultural operation. She also controls over the rearing, use and disposal of domestic animals. Thus she has considerable control over the livelihood of the household. Despite the customary practice of inheriting land through the male line, Angami women do inherit land as gift from their parents especially at the time of marriage. This implies changes in the system of land which eventually affects land relations and pattern of inheritance. Women's right to land is partially recognized, though the right to use has been there since time immemorial. However, patriarchal ethos is still looming large. For instance, there are unresolved questions relating to inheritance of land, specially acquired land, and women who are married outside the village, but not necessarily outside the state. Should they be treated as daughters of the village or outsiders? Do they cease to be the daughters of their parents once they are married? My point is, landed property can never be shifted to another place and incase of transfer of ownership, it is still transfer within the village. Whoever it may belong to, the land is part of the village and it will be, as long as the village exist. And any more arguments over the matter imply that the age-old practice of women inheriting the mother's fields or acquiring acquired property of the parents among this group of Angami holds no ground.

Finally observations made among the Angamis may be found in other tribal groups as well. For example, among the *Konyaks* of Mon district, traditionally women do not inherit land, according to some women I personally interacted with. But there are several cases where more enlightened parents have gifted land to their daughters. There are variations in the customs and practices of the different groups of this tribe and may be some studies can be done in the near future.

This is one of the most unfortunate aspects of tribal people in the region and factors like education, occupation and religion do not seem to have had any success towards overcoming such gender biases among men ... but it is not enough to talk about reservations or blame patriarchy. Women must make a concerted effort to change their destiny (Zehol 2003: 301). Customary laws and traditional values have always favoured patriarchy and has been in existence since time immemorial. Therefore, it is next to impossible to do away with patriarchy and patrilineal system. Men and women are different by nature, and therefore they cannot be treated equally on the basis of uniformity but, surely there is enough and more space to treat them as persons having rights and duties. Thereby complementing each other and this definitely requires genuine efforts from both men and women to create a society where each person is given opportunities to live a fuller life.

REFERENCES

1. Bareh, Hamlet; 1993; 'India's North-East and Her Ethnic Character during the British and Contemporary Setup' in B. Pakem (ed.), *Regionalism in India;* New Delhi; Har-Anand Publications.

2. Deeney, John and Walter Fernandes; 1992; 'Tribals: Their Dependence on Forests, Their Traditions and Management Systems' in Walter Fernandes (ed.), *National Development and Tribal Deprivations;* New Delhi; Indian Social Institute.

3. D'Souza, Alphonsus; 1999; *North East India*; Jakhama; Kohima Jesuit Region (Mimeo).

4. ______________ 2001; *Traditional Systems of Forest Conservation in North East India: The Angami Tribe of Nagaland;* Guwahati; North Eastern Social Science Research Centre.

5. D'Souza, Alphonsus, Christina Kekhrieseno & Veronica Nokhwenu; 2002; *Status of Women in North East India: A Comparative Study of Three Ethnic Groups in North- East India (Aka, Angami and Dimasa);* Jakhama; St Joseph's College (mimeo).

6. Epstein, Cynthia Fuchs; 1988; *Descriptive Distinction: Sex Gender and the Social Order;* New Haven; Yale University. Press.

7. Fernandes, Walter, Gita Bharali & Vimedo Kezo; 2008; *The UN Indigeneous Decade in Northeast India;* Guwahati; North Eastern Social Science Research Centre.

8. Hutton, J.H; 1921; *The Angami Naga;* London; Macmillan & Co. Reprinted 1969; Bombay; Oxford University Press.

9. Haimendorf, Von Christopher; 1939; *The Naked Nagas*; London; Methuen & Co.

10. Kekhrieseno, Christina; 2007; 'Changing Land Relations in Angami Society', paper presented at the seminar on *The Angami Society at the Beginning of 21st Century;* Kigwema; Japfü Christian College, November 28-29.

11. Elwin, Verrier; 1969; *The Nagas in the Nineteenth Century;* Bombay; Oxford University Press.

12. Pathy, Jaganath; 1988; *Ethnic Minorities in the Process of Development;* Jaipur; Rawat Publications.

13. Saxena, Poonam Pradhan; 1991; 'Property Rights of women under the Indian Succession Act, 1925' in Shamsuddin Shama (ed.), *Women, Law and Social Change;* New Delhi; Ashish Publishing House.

14. Sivaramayya, B; 1991; 'Women's access to Land and Other Productive Resources. Legislative Policy of Hunting with Hounds and Running with Hare' in Shamsuddin Shama (ed.), *Women, Law and Social Change;* New Delhi; Ashish Publishing House.

15. Sema, Piketo; 1992; *British Policy and Administration in Nagaland: 1881-1947;* New Delhi; Scholar Publishing House.

16. Scott, William P; 1999; *Dictionary of Sociology (Special Indian Edition);* New Delhi; Goyal Saab.

17. Zehol, Vashum Lucy; 2003; 'Status of Tribal Women' in T.B. Subha and G.C. Ghosh (ed.), *The Anthropology of North-East India;* New Delhi; Orient Longman.

18. Gazetteer of India; 1970; *Nagaland: Kohima District;* Kohima; Govt. of India.

9

Khiamniungan Women: The Changing Status

N.S. Khaikho

[The study of women is gaining importance in recent years with its basic goal to gather information on women to gain insight about their multifarious roles and problems. The ultimate objective is to empower women in their struggle against marginality and inequality prevalent in the society.

The present paper is an attempt to present the challenges and problems faced by the Khiamniungan women and also to highlight the changing status of the women from traditional to modernity. But unfortunately we do not have much knowledge about the life of Khiamniungan women in particular and the Khiamniungan as a whole, due to lack of research studies and absence of relevant literatures on them. In fact no research has been done on them so far. Therefore, this paper related to Khiamniungan women will be the first of its kind which attempts to present their changing roles and status in a descriptive form. The paper is based on data gathered through interviews, observation during the field visit, group discussions and related secondary materials.]

Nagaland is a tiny, beautiful, land locked, mountainous state of North-East India sharing its boundaries with Myanmar and Arunachal Pradesh in the east, Assam in the west, Assam and Arunachal Pradesh in the north and Manipur in the south. Nagaland State is predominantly a tribal State and is a home for sixteen major tribes namely Angami, Ao, Chakeshang, Chang,

Khiamniungan, Kuki, Konyak, Kachari, Lotha, Phom, Pochury, Rengma, Sumi, Sangtam, Yimchungru and Zeliang. Traditionally Naga society is a patriarchal or male dominated society and women are subordinate to man but compared with their counterparts in more civilized parts of India the Naga women enjoy greater privileges and status.

Khiamniungan: Land and People

Khiamniungan is one the major tribe in Nagaland and yet happens to be one of the lesser known tribe among the Nagas. The Khiamniungan as a distinct tribal group occupies the eastern most part of Nagaland under Tuensang district and north western part of Myanmar. Unfortunately, the birth of India in 1947 followed by official visit of the two Prime Ministers, Jawaharlal Nehru and Thakin Nu (U Nu) in 1953 divided the land of the Khiamniungans forcing them to live in two countries. Even though they are living in two countries due to divide and rule policy adopted by the colonizers, Khiamniungans belongs to one family and share common history and culture. Presently there are 36 Khiamniungan villages in India and160 villages in Myanmar.

The Khiamniungan villages in Myanmar are divided into four ranges namely Thingniu range, Thyak range, Longpai range and Kondon range. The land largely unknown and unvisited by the outside world and far from modern civilization is tucked away in the north-western corner of Myanmar under Upper Sagaing Division (Central administrative area) along the International border of India. Their land stretches from the foothills of Patkai range to the plains of Chinwin River.

Traditional Role and Status of Khiamniungan Women

Like all other Naga tribes, Khiamniungan society is also a male dominated society and women are largely excluded from decision making. Women are not allowed to participate in most of the social gatherings and religious ceremonies, they are not even allowed to venture near the vicinity of Morung (Kamnoi) where men folk gather to make important decisions. Women are restricted to household work i.e. cooking, cleaning, child bearing, child rearing etc. They are considered to be weak, vulnerable and dependent on men, and yet they run the households, while men deal with outside works and assistance only. Despite the marginalization of women in the social and the religious aspect, the contribution of women in the economic activities cannot be undermined. She is an equal partner of her husband in his economic pursuit.

The division of labour between the sexes is guided by practical considerations. Men usually do the tough jobs and leave such works to women which need less physical strain but much endurance. Thus, while cutting of forest is done by the men, the women remove the shrubs and other small growth. Men burn the field, remove trees and leave the job of sowing and periodic cleaning of weeds in the field to women. Women's contribution in the domestic affairs provides her a more secured place in the family and leaves her with no time for other activities. She wakes up before dawn and pounds rice, fetches water, cook and feed the family, after meal she proceeds to the field and works the whole day. She returns from the field at dusk, usually with a load of firewood and fodder for domestic animals and on reaching home she has to start cooking for the evening meal and at night when the family members rest, she stays awake spinning yarn and weaving cloths. In all these she is assisted by the girl child. Despite the fact that men are responsible for protection of village and perform tougher jobs, women are over burdened with work from dawn till dusk leaving very little room for leisure time.

Status of a Girl Child

There is no doubt that in a Khiamniungan society a male child is given more importance and is considered as an asset to the family more than a girl child due to the patrilineal system where ancestry is traced through male line, property and status is passed on from the father to legitimate son. The birth of a girl child is never considered as a misfortune or a curse, rather the girl child is welcomed as an extra hand to help their parent in the family. Since agriculture was the main occupation requiring maximum man-power, therefore, the Khiamniungans prefer big family so that they will have enough man power to cultivate the field. The girl child is never discriminated and receives good treatment in the family except that they don't have the right over inheritance and property.

Marriage and Divorce

Polygamy is not an accepted form of marriage in the Khiamniungan society. Early marriage is also not encouraged in the Khiamniungan society. 20 to 25 years is considered as the right age for marriage for both boys and girls, the reason is that once married, a couple is expected to establish their own home therefore, the children have an obligation to serve their parent during their best years. The youngest male child remains at the ancestral home and is also responsible for taking care of the aged parents.

Marriage in traditional Khiamniungan society is more of a social obligation for reproduction and continuation of generation and does not have any religious significance. Both love and arrange marriages are common but marriage within the same clan is a taboo (strictly exogamy). Khiamniungans also practice a unique custom of marriage which other Naga tribes normally do not practice i.e. abduction of bride which was an accepted way of life, but before abducting a girl, the boy along with his friends spy on her so as to ascertain her family background and also to know whether she will be a good wife. If the boy is convinced that she will be compatible to him, he along with his friends goes to her house and abducts her, the girls parent usually remain as a helpless spectator. The girl is then kept at the boy's house for two to three days, during this period if the girl still remains adamant and refuses to settle with him, the girl is allowed to return back to her parent but if the girl accepts and decides to live with him then the marriage is solemnized through a simple ritual in the presence of the boy's family. A chicken is beheaded, and then its blood is mixed with rice beer in a cup made of banana leave. The girl dips her index finger in the cup and swears to live faithfully; similarly the boy also dips his index finger and swears to be loyal. From that moment they are pronounced as husband and wife. The bride is then allowed to go to her parent's house to collect her belongings.

Divorce is as simple as marriage. It may be initiated by either party for reasons such as incompatibility, adultery, disease, childlessness or quarrel. The husband can simply order the wife out and severe all matrimonial ties or the wife could simply walk out of the house taking along only her belongings. However, in Pangsha a plot of land and household property is given to the other party depending on who has divorced. After divorce a women has the right to remarry again.

The Present Status of Khiamniungan Women

Compared with other Naga tribes, Khiamniungans were exposed to modern civilization very late. When the rest of the country was embarking upon education and modernization, the people of this area were in a totally different world, clinging to their age-old customs and practices. The Khiamniungans experienced a tremendous speed of change in all spheres of life with the advent of Christianity in 1947 followed by the introduction of formal educational institutions. The rapid process of modernization has brought overwhelming change in the social and economic life of the people which has both positive and negative impact on the women.

Women and Christianity

Christianity as a religion advocates equality and respect for women. With the coming of Christianity and conversion from male oriented animist religion of the Khiamniungan, the womenfolk had more privileges and opportunity to participate in church activities and religious affairs. The age old custom of abduction of bride is no longer practiced; marriages are solemnized in church giving due importance and security to women's position in the family. Yet even in church the major decision making is vested with the deacon board consisting of only men therefore, apart from participating in religious activities the women are marginalized when it comes to decision making.

Education and Women

Initially when schools were established, education for girls was not encouraged and so while their brothers go to school the girl child remains at home taking care of household chores and field work along with their parents. Thus, men took the opportunity to avail the urban as well as modern opportunities while majority of women remained illiterate and confined in their rural home.

Times are changing and today's parents have realized the importance of girl child and are giving due importance for their education reducing the gender disparity in education. These days young Khiamniungan women are not just satisfied with their traditional roles of housekeeping, they are more ambitious and career oriented than their male counterpart. Compared with men very few women are employed in public and private sectors. Yet majority of rural women still face the problem of illiteracy, poor education facilities, poor economy etc. and also struggles to manage the balance between career and family, personal decisions and prioritizing the needs.

Women and Health

The Khiamniungan area is still under-developed and lacks basic infrastructure like road connectivity to every village and communication facilities. Even the existing road connectivity is poorly maintained which in turn has an adverse effect on women. The existence of low literacy rate especially among the rural women hinders the process of communicating the issue of health, sanitation and hygiene. Women face a greater health risk than men, particularly during child birth. Nearly 70% of rural women do not have access to medical facilities. Most of the villages do not have proper health care centre and lacks trained medical personnel. In the absence of trained nurses most of the child deliveries are conducted by untrained person causing injuries to both mother and child and even leading to death due to lack of knowledge to tackle complicated case such as placental retention and excessive bleeding which could be easily tackled by a trained nurse. Transportation of serious cases of women during deliveries with complications is hampered due to lack of proper road connectivity and transportation facilities leading to loss of precious lives. The only referral hospital in Khiamniungan area is Community Health Centre at Noklak but there is no proper equipment for operation and no X-ray facility. Moreover, there is no gynaecologist posted at CHC, Noklak to tackle the increasing women health problems. Most of the women in rural area cannot afford to go outside for treatment due to financial constraints.

The lack of awareness for family planning combined with rural economy based on primitive agricultural practices requiring maximum man-power which are family oriented has serious consequences on women. A woman spends nearly 70% of her married life in child bearing and lactation.

Khiamniungan Women in Myanmar

The overall scenario of Khiamniungan women in Myanmar is pathetic. The Khiamniungan villages in Myanmar remains isolated from all modern means of transport and communication and the people are still semi-nomadic surviving with bare essentials of life. These villages do not have access to medical facilities due to the absence of dispensaries and trained medical personnel in their villages, which have serious consequences on the health of the women in particular and the whole community at large. Another major problem faced by the people is the abuse of human right violation by the Burmese army. The Burmese army visits each village twice or trice in a year and during such time, the villagers are forced to act as their porter irrespective of sex and age. The villagers are also forced to work in road constructions, repairing military camps in Khamti and Lahe town for months together disrupting the normal life of the villagers. In all these the women suffer the most. The literacy rate is also very low which further aggravates their problem. They don't have any platform to air their grievances. The scenario in Myanmar will remain bleak as long as the present Military Junta remains in power.

The parents in order to protect their children from military persecution and in the hope for better future send their children especially through middle man across the border to Indian side for education. Every year hundreds of such children come to India and most of them end up as domestic helpers who are scattered all over Nagaland. Many parents are not aware where their kids are staying and how they are doing. In the wake of the recent increase in human trafficking cases from North-East, such children from across the border especially girls are at risk. So far there are no voluntary organizations to monitor the welfare of those children from Myanmar.

Conclusion

Khiamniungan women are still lagging behind men and have little or no influence in the decision-making in religious, political, social or economic issues. In this regard, women empowerment can be accelerated by making them self-reliant and contributing their self-earned resources to the family. Women's economic empowerment is absolutely essential for raising their status and for active participation in decision making.

At present there is a need to establish voluntary organizations to address the issues and problem faced by the women. The Khiamniungan Mother's Association (Mele Menyiu Hoikam) was started only in March, 2008 and may take sometime to make its impact. There is an urgent need to generate awareness for women's right to good health and control over fertility which could enhance the life span of women and creation of infrastructure of primary health care to give them access to modern health care. One should realize that a healthy mother reflects a healthy society. The mind controls the body and health is determined to a great extent by education. It is obvious that a literate mother has better access to the health care system and can better look after herself and her family. For and overall development of a society it is crucial to enlighten, educate and empower women. Khiamniungan women have to emerge as agents of social, political and economic change in the society.

REFERENCES

1. Ghosh, Lipi, Ishita Mukhopadhyay & Suchandra Chakraborty (ed.); 2008; *Women Across Asia: Issues of Identity*; New Delhi; Gyan Publishing House.
2. Kumar, B.B; 1998; *Society and Culture in a Corner of Nagaland;* Meerut; Pragati Prakashan.

3. Kumari, Sumitra; 2006; *Dynamic of Women Empowerment*; New Delhi; Alfa Publications.

4. Rao, Digumarti Bhaskara and Digumarti Pushpalatha Rao (ed.); 1999; *Women Challenges and Advancement*; New Delhi; Discovery Publishing House.

5. Sardeshpande, S.C; 1987; *The Patkoi Nagas*; Delhi; Daya Publishing House.

6. Seth, Mera; 2004; *Women and Development: The Indian Experience*; New Delhi; Sage Publications.

7. Shashi, S.S; 1978; *The Tribal Women of India*; Delhi; Sundeep Prakashan.

10

Women Emancipation in Angami Society

Koseno

The Angamis are one of the Naga tribes who are the principal inhabitants of Nagaland. Hutton (1921:15) and Das (1994:63) identified four distinct groups among the Angamis. They are the Khonoma group, Kohima group, Viswema group and the Chakroma group. At present, it is common to identify them on the basis of their geographical distribution. Those living in Kohima and the villages surrounding it are the Northern Angamis, the Western Angamis and the Southern Angamis.

The data given are taken out from the Research Work *'Changing Role and Status of Educated Angami Women.'*

Today's world by and large is comparatively a rapid changing one and the change has been in a variety of directions. Socially, one of the most remarkable changes brought about in recent history has been the comparative emancipation of womankind – its emergence from the exclusive seclusion of the home into the world. With the growth of literacy rate, the society's attitude in relation to women has broadened a great deal. She is no more given a bias treatment because of being a woman. Education has made a mother an earner of livelihood, which boosts up the women's moral and social standing. The wife or the mother need not necessarily confine herself to the household drudgery but freely engage herself in other social and economic matters as her competency and abilities render her fit. Women's education and employment play a pivotal role in initiating the far-reaching changes in every social structure. Thus, due to their changed social standing in the society women even decide matters relating to different spheres of life. Most of the educated women go for gainful employment to a great extent due to economic necessity, whereby they raise their social status in the society.

The importance of educated women's role and status in the society has completely changed during the past few decades. It is no longer a question of what women are capable of doing physically and mentally. Experience has settled the long controversy about feminine abilities and proved that women are fit for much wider range of activities than the traditional role of housewife. Marriage and work for educated women are of great social interest and importance in the present day urban societies of India. Women working outside their homes are not a new phenomenon because women in rural India have always been working for a living in the fields along with their men. Taking up of employment by the educated middle class and upper class women is comparatively a recent phenomenon. Even the married women are coming out of the four walls of their homes seeking gainful employment. The degree of freedom given to women to move about in society and to take part in public life gives a good idea of the nature of the changing role and status in the society. It has enabled us to realize the truth that women too have a contribution of their own for development and progress. It is evident that women's role and status have been changing due to educational opportunity provided to them. They started taking multiple roles and work equally with their male counterparts. Their exposure to various fields have broadened their outlooks and carried out new ideas of social developments. They have changed their attitudes regarding marriage, occupations, family and also decision-making. With the attainment of Independence in 1947, the socio-economic transformation in Indian societies has brought about a train of economic transformation and a train of perceptible change in Indian societies, which also have touched the Angami society. It has specifically affected the status, role, outlook, world view and the attitudes of the educated Angami women to a great extent.

The traditional occupation of a woman was either to be a housewife, a mother or farmer because of the strong social stand that a girl's duty was to work and not to earn and the girl child remained illiterate. The basically patriarchal Naga society is reflected by the notion that the birth of a male child was considered auspicious, man as the breadwinner and protector of the society and women being subordinate to their husbands. However, the progressive modernization brought by the adoption of Christianity and spread of education has gradually altered the contemporary situation among the Naga women. Lucy Zehol (1998) in her book *Status of Naga Women* provides information on the status of Angami women. It provides that looking back to the bygone generation, *thenumia* (women) have been confined to the four walls of the house.

However, with the passage of time, she is given more liberty even in other spheres of life, apart from her household chores. Mills (1969) aptly states that their roles and duties in the traditional society were "to weave clothing required for the family, work in the fields, cut and bring in firewood and perform all manners of drudgery". In the traditional days, 'women', whether wife, daughter, sister or mother was made to feel inferior to men. As a wife or mother, she was all in-charge of the household chores. She was expected to stay close at home and learn the household chores. A daughter was seldom encouraged to study. In fact, there were many cases where the daughter was totally prohibited to attend school in spite of her abilities and desire to learn. This was so because education was seen as a means of making girls go way ward and unhomely. With the progress in the field of education, more and more women are becoming salaried wives and daughters. The conservative view has slackened giving more scope to girl education (Zehol, 1998). Today a woman in salaried job is not looked down upon as crossing the social norms as was the case in the past. They have equal privileges to work equally with men in all walks of life. The expected role of a mother goes beyond the home and upbringing of her children. She is expected to share the responsibilities of development of society in all its facets.

It is, therefore, found that education leads to alienation from home-making role. The expanded educational opportunities available to girls have served to make them less satisfied with their traditional home-making role. There is considerable evidence that many women, having been encouraged by education to think like men, find home-making to be relatively unstimulating. Education exposes to new thoughts and ideas which provides necessary skills. Education has made them to occupy permanent and secured services with better income. It is found that no educated woman likes to work inside the home; instead, they prefer to move out and work together with men than to work with the same sex. Most of them are satisfied with their present job working upto their expectation, which is a clear indication of having good placement in their jobs. Whereas, the traditional women were to engage themselves with the domestic works of fetching the firewood, draw the water, cook the food and brew liquor besides working in the fields and weaving cloths at home. The modern women make themselves occupied in various works in spite of having secured economy at home. Economic necessity is not the only motive for taking up or continuing their jobs. It is found that even those educated women whose parents or husbands have quite handsome incomes are found to be in various jobs, which are not even well-paid. They work in order to enhance their social status. Most of the educated women get freedom to be employed in various occupations. They take up jobs of their choice with their own initiatives without prior approval of their husbands.

It is found that today even husbands, relatives, parents and even members of the old generation approves, or do not mind the educated daughter, wife and daughter-in-law working and rather encourages them that they should help the family by supplementing its income and also raise their own social status in the society. The fact revealed by various data collected indicates that today educated women are working or in employment not because they are forced or compelled by their parents, husbands, as it used to be, but also because they themselves want to work due to various other socio-psychological motivations and interests. This is a vital change in their attitudes towards their individual status as well as towards a significant social change. The participation of women in employment outside home has greatly changed their family lives. The most far-reaching effect has been the economic independence attained by working women and redistribution of the work within the family, where they can still participate in their work while continuing many of their traditional familial obligations. The tasks previously assigned to the wife are being assumed or shared by the husband and wife jointly so that the wife can have equal responsibility for earning the family living. The employment of women may be viewed as a cause for a decrease in the differentiation of sex roles. When a woman works she presumably increases her ability to sanction or control, because of the financial contribution she makes to the family. The modern educated women want her say to be implemented in the family. She wants to involve herself in the decisions at least regarding children's education, budgeting and financial matters, whereas in the traditional-bound Angami society man is the head of the household and he makes most of the decisions.

The employment and education of women have given them resources, which their unemployed counterparts do not have. The salary or income of working women is a substantial contribution to the family income, which would be expected to give her greater interest in financial decision and greater respect from her husband and other members of the family. The participation of the women in the activities of the outside world through her job gives her contact with fellow-workers, which lessens her dependence on her husband for emotional support and increases the knowledge and skill she brings to decision-making. Such factors have made them resourceful and competent decision-makers.

REFERENCES

1. Hutton, J. H.. 1969; *The Angami Nagas* (second edition); New Delhi; Macmillan & Co.
2. Mills, A. J; 1969; 'Military Expedition to the Angami Naga Hills' in Verrier Elwin (ed.), *The Nagas in the Nineteenth Century*; London; Oxford University Press.
3. Zehol, Lucy., 1998; *Women in Naga Society*; New Delhi; Regency Publications.

11

Border-Trade among the Lotha Women and the Ahoms

Lichumo Enie

Introduction

The Lotha Nagas are one of the major Naga tribe found in Nagaland. The Lothas belong to the Indo-Mongoloid race speaking the dialects belonging to the Sino-Tibetan family (Tibeto-Burman) of languages. The Lothas live in Wokha district which is bounded by the districts of Mokokchung in the North, Zunheboto in the East, Kohima in the South and the State of Assam in the West. In the pre-colonial days each Lotha Naga occupied its own specific territory and was grouped into a number of villages and each village occupied a well marked area. There are no land records but boundary disputes are extremely rare (Murkot Ramunny, p. 2).

Wokha is inhabited by the Lotha Nagas, located at 26.1° N 94.27° E with an area of 1,628 sq. km. According to 2001 India census, the area of Wokha district has a population of 1,61,098. Men constitute about 51.92 % while women constitute 48.08 % of the population of Wokha. The summer temperature of Wokha district is between 16.1° C and 32° C. The winter temperature is a 2° C minimum. The rainfall of Wokha is between 2 and 2.5 meters per year.

The Lotha villages were self-governing units. Traffic and trade between villages were minimal as a result each village grew in isolation. The Lotha Nagas living in the border areas had economic links with the Ahoms. Historical records like the *Buranjis* also gives us an insight about the Naga history. According to the sources there was trade and commerce relation between the Nagas and the people of the plains as early as the thirteenth century, as the *Buranjis* mentions of the Ahom Kingdom that started in this century.

Most of the Lotha Nagas, who lived on the low lands close to the plains, did so due to the economic reasons. The Lotha women had long been carrying out trade with the Ahoms of the Assam valley. Lotha women from the Changpang, Tssori, Yingsung, Bhandari, Yamhon, Longchum, Pangti, Lakhuti villages ventured to the foothills to do trade with the Ahoms. The women would often accompany their menfolk carrying their commodities in their different baskets like *pharu,* meant for vegetables and firewood, *okhyak* meant for carrying rice, *yenpha* meant for journeys specially on marketing, to the lands granted to them by the Ahoms also known as Naga-khats, in the foot hills and did business with the Ahoms. The lands granted to them were accorded with the condition, that the Lotha would not raid the plains and they would have the right to collect tax from the Naga-khats. Thus, trade was carried out under the Ahom king survey and also provided security to the Ahoms as well.

The plots of land allotted to the Lotha Nagas later became the permanent market place. The common market place where the Lotha women ventured were Rajapar, Furkating, Borholla, Titapur, Tokenegara. Jorhat, Golaghat and later Merapani, also known as Maraju to the Lothas. *It is to be noted that Merapani was not a market place initially but rather a land mark or a resting place for them on their way to the Ahom valleys. Merapani developed as a market place only in the later years. At present the place is thickly populated by Muslims.*

Earlier there was very little trade except in some beads and shells (Hargovind Joshi, p. 54). But in the later part the women traded in cotton and black sesames, ginger, dried chilies, bamboo crafts, brinjal, yarn, betal nuts and leaves, yam, wet and dried bamboo shoots, and agricultural implements. At times ivory and animal skin was also traded but it was on a limited scale and only few people did business with it. Since the Lothas did not use any kind of medium therefore, barter system was the only method of trade. They usually exchanged their commodities with salt, iron, dried fish, pan leaves, palm-leaf mats, gourds, duck, rice, hen, cows, coal, jute, cowrie shells, brass wire and metal sheets etc from the Ahoms. In addition the plains provided ornaments produced particularly for the Naga market. Among the commodities salt was the most important item which appears to have been traded in a circular way. The women would carry the salt to their villages and sell it to the other neighboring Naga villages. The cattle imported from the plains were vital for sacrifices and ceremonial feast (Julian Jacobs, pg34). The Lotha also used to sell the cattle acquired from the plains to the neighbouring Aos and Sema Nagas, through barter system (K.S. Singh, p. 117).

Value of Commodities

1. 1 kg of cotton was exchanged with 15 kg of salt.
2. 10 kg of black sesame was exchanged with 30 kg of salt.
3. 1 kg of chilli was exchanged with 3 kg of dry fish.

Value of Money

The Ahoms used money which was made of brass

1. 1 kg of cotton is equivalent to 5 shorota or 5 kg of salt.
2. 1 kg of black sesame is equivalent to 3 shorota or 3 kg of salt.
3. 1 kg of dried chilli was 8 moya.

Before the advent of the British, most of the goods would have been exchanged through the barter system. There were some items, however, which resembled money type objects. Brass discs, wooden or metal spear-shaped objects called Chabili and shell or bone strings served the function of the widely recognized standard medium of exchange. So at times the women sold their commodities and with the money they bought their daily requirements. Payment was made either in cash or in kind (K.S. Singh, p. 116). The proper use of money as a medium of exchange was introduced only by the colonial administrator and hence, there was no significant monetized system of trade in the Pre-British period (Piketo Sema, p. 133). Trade and commerce which were insignificant during the Pre-colonial period received impetus with the introduction of British administration. It was only in the later part that trade was carried out in an extensive manner making it their main profession. Especially with the introduction of the British administration, the traditional system of trading has been replaced by the more efficient and systematic manner.

A kind of bilingualism was in vogue amongst the hill tribes, especially among those of their members who had to maintain contacts with the plains-folks and carry on their business. The latter too had known the tribal dialects sufficiently enough to be able to carry on conversation with the hill people. So knowledge of Assamese had to be acquired by the visiting tribesmen by way of necessity and the same case with the people of the plains who had to carry on trade or transact business of the state (Suryakumar Bhuyan, p. 53). Means of communication was Nagamese. It was started only after the allotment of the markets, also known as the Naga-khats.

The regular contacts that existed between the Lothas and the Ahoms have introduced new need into their life and to some extend modified the daily round. Further, the introduction of a monetary medium of exchange, which has been going on for a century, has tended to alter indigenous standards of wealth.

The basic unit of the Lotha family was based on the patriarchal form of society where the male is the head of the family and women were subordinate to man. Customary laws also permitted man to have rights and freedoms from which women were excluded. But the women taking part in the economic life of the society was unique. Women broke through their restrictions from the society and ventured to the plains as far as taking them three to four days to reach certain Naga-khats. It was never because of poverty that the women accompanied their men to the Naga-khats facing dangers from head hunters and wild animals but at the same time it was natural urge and their adventurous nature that led to an astounding development not new to the men folks. Thus, the women played an important role in the trade and commerce along with their men as they ventured to the Naga-khats.

REFERENCES

1. Bendangangshi; 1993; *Glimpse of the Naga History*; Guwahati; Saraighat Offset Press.
2. Bhuyan, Suryankumar; 1949; *Anglo- Assamese Relations 1771-1826*; Guwahati; Lawyer's Book Stall.
3. ________________ 1965; *Studies in the History of Assam*; New Delhi; Omsons Publications.
4. Butler, John; 1994; *Travels in Assam*; Delhi; Manas Publications.
5. Gait, Edward; 2003; *A History of Assam*; Delhi; Surjeet Publications.
6. Goswami, Surendra Kumar; 1981; *A History of Revenue Administration in Assam (1228 - 1826 A.D): A Detailed History of the Revenue System of the Ahom Rulers*; Guwahati; Spectrum Publications.
7. Hutton, J.H; 1995; *Diaries of Two Tours in the Unadministered Area East of the Naga Hills*; New Delhi; Mittal Publications.
8. Jacobs, Julian; 1990; *The Nagas, Hill People of North East India Society, Culture and the Colonial Encounters*; Thames and Hudson.
9. Joshi, Hargovind; 2001; *Nagaland: Past and Present*; New Delhi; Akansha Publishing House.
10. Mackenzie, Alexander; 2004; *The North East Frontier of India*; New Delhi; Mittal Publications.
11. Nuh, V.K; 2002; *The Naga Chronicle*; New Delhi; Regency Publication.
12. Ramunny, Murkot; 1988; *The World of Nagas*; New Delhi; Northern Book Centre.
13. Reid, Robert; 1983; *History of the Frontier areas Bordering on Assam 1883-1941*; Delhi; Eastern Publishing House.
14. Sema, Hokishe; 1986; *Emergence of Nagaland, Socioeconomic and Political Transformation and the Future*; New Delhi; Vikas Publishing House Pvt. Ltd.
15. Sema, Piketo; 1991; *British Policy and Administration in Nagaland (1881- 1947)*; New Delhi; Scholar Publishing House.

12

Women and Crime: A Sociological Examination of Women Criminals in Nagaland

M. Temjen Longkumer

Introduction

Crime statistics in India indicates that female or women criminality in India is not a significant problem. This is also found to be true in case of Nagaland. However, when the rate of female crimes is found to be low, we can definitely say that the nature and intensity of female crimes have become more serious and complex when we consider its trend for the past one to two decades. For instance, from 3.1 per cent (of the total crimes committed in India) in 1990, female crimes under the Indian Penal Code increased to 3.5 per cent in 1992 and 5.4 per cent in 1998.[1] Therefore, an attempt is made to study the women criminals of Nagaland in particular.

Conceptual Framework

Any woman or a female member of a society who commits crime or an offence may be called as a woman criminal. Crime may be defined as an anti-social behavior that has violated public sentiments to such an extent as to be forbidden by statute.[2] In other words, crime is an act forbidden by the law of the land, and one which is considered sufficiently serious to warrant providing penalties for its commission.[3] In strict sociological terms, crime may be simply defined as an act or behavior if it hurts or harms the sentiments of the general public of that particular community whether such acts are against the written law of the land or not.

Methodology and Area of Study

This piece of work is based on a quantitative type of study with an empirical approach. Data have been collected both from secondary as well as primary sources. The secondary data have been collected from local dailies (Newspaper reports) and relevant literature. Primary data have been collected by personally interviewing the women prisoners.

Thus, the present work is based on a study of 3 major jails in Nagaland including Central Jail, Dimapur; Sub-Jail, Dimapur and District Jail, Kohima. In order to get the ratio of male-female inmates (or criminals), Central Jail, Dimapur was considered otherwise it does not house any female inmates. Therefore, prisoners' interview was conducted only at Sub-Jail, Dimapur and District Jail, Kohima.

Findings of the Study

According to the study, male offenders (95.15%) in Nagaland outnumbered female offenders (4.84%) with a large margin which shows that male members of the society are more likely to commit crime. It also indicates that female members of the society are less problematic and have lesser tendency to commit crime.

Whatever may be the rate of female criminals and the seriousness of female criminality, a sociological examination of women/female criminals in Nagaland indicates the following implications.

Age

Taken at an interval of ten digits, it is found that the age-group between 36-45 (inclusive) accounts for the highest number of female prisoners constituting 44 per cent of the total respondents, followed by age-group of 26-35 with 36 per cent while 46 and above constitutes 12 per cent. Interestingly, the younger age-group of 16-25 accounts for only 8 per cent constituting the lowest percentage. It indicates that while young and older women are less likely to commit crime, marriageable age or married women and child bearing stage have higher tendency to commit crime.

Marital Status

It is found that majority of the female prisoners (80%) are married while the divorce rate from among the married women is found to be 32 per cent. Thus, we can conclude that married women are more likely to commit crime in society (in particular reference to Nagaland). From among the respondents (female inmates), 25 per cent of them are also found to be widows. This finding, further, supports the above given statement (made under *Age* category) that woman of marriageable age or married and child bearing stages have a higher tendency to commit crime in society.

Educational Status

With regards to educational attainment, majority of the respondents (58.33%) are found to be under matric (class X), while rest of them (41.66%) are either illiterate or uneducated. It clearly shows that almost all of the female criminals who attended formal education are school drop outs because none of the respondents are found to be studying beyond matriculation.

Economic Status

As regards to their monthly income, majority of the respondents (41.66%) income falls below Rs. 2000, followed by 33.33 per cent whose income is nil. While 16.66 per cent of them fall under 2000-5000 income group, only 8.33 per cent are found to be earning between 5000 and 10,000. Therefore, we can conclude that female criminals, particularly in Nagaland, generally come from a lower income group.

Occupational Status

From among the respondents, 66.66 per cent are found to be earning by themselves while rest of them (33.33%) are unemployed who do not earn anything. However, their occupations include LDA/clerical job, tailoring, massager, dai (IV grade worker in hospital), farmer, petty business (trade and commerce), etc. Their occupational structure also indicates that they generally belong to a lower income group.

Nature of Crimes Committed

Basing on the respondents of the study, some of the nature of crimes committed by women in Nagaland includes ganja smuggling, kidnapping and child trafficking, murder of husband, murder other than husband, drug addiction, prostitution, crime against public order, theft, robbery, burglary, heroin smuggling, arms smuggling and rape conspiracy.

Considering the various nature of crimes committed by women in Nagaland, it is found that besides other minor factors, women criminals in Nagaland commit crimes for two main reasons: money and unhealthy or hostile relationships with primary kin.

In crimes like ganja smuggling, kidnapping and child trafficking, prostitution, theft, robbery, burglary, heroin and arms smuggling, it is found that crime is committed either for want of money (in cases like kidnapping, child trafficking, prostitution and robbery) or material gains (theft and burglary), and for commission money (in cases like ganja, heroin and arms smuggling).

On the other hand, it is found that murder of husband, drug addiction and in some cases, even prostitution are committed due to unfriendly and hostile relationships among the primary members of family including one's husband.

Prostitution

Prostitution can be one of the most common crimes committed by women criminals everywhere. This offence requires the participation of a 'customer' (almost always a male) who purchases the opportunity to engage in that behavior/act. Such regulation would come under Immoral Traffic Prevention Act.

Prostitution or 'flesh trade', dubbed as the world's oldest profession and though such activities are prohibited by law (though legalized in some countries), the offenders still follow it as a profession to earn their livelihood in most cases.

As per reports, majority of the accused are non-locals/non-Nagas though even Naga women are arrested at times for such immoral activities. In some cases, even married women are also involved. Offenders are mostly arrested by the women cell of the police department and sometimes by factional groups while conducting raids in hotels.[4]

According to a study, done by a newspaper reporter, local girls in sex trade belong to various communities including Adivasis, Assamese, Nepalese and Bangladeshis (mostly illegal migrants) and Nagas. Types of women involved in sex trade include single, married, divorcee and widow with or without children who are drug users and whose husbands are drunkards. While majority of them are forced into the trade for economic reason, some got influenced by friends and some by their own choice.[5]

Observation and Suggestions

From the above discussion, it can be said that women criminals in Nagaland commit crimes for two main reasons: i) money and ii) unhealthy or hostile relationships with members of primary kin.

Findings of the study indicate that most of the women criminals belong to higher age-group and at the same time, majority are married. Therefore, besides giving proper guidance at an early age, continuous moral education should be imparted. When criminals are found to be married, it indicates defective family system or hostile and unfriendly relationships among family members. Therefore, proper family counseling including conflict resolution should be given to such criminals. Various

Non-Governmental Organizations (NGOs) and Church or religious workers can be a great help in this area.

Majority of the woman criminals are found to be either uneducated/illiterate or below matric which indicates that lower the educational attainment, higher the crime rate. It can be suggested that women education and literacy should be given importance both at the family level and public life.

Majority of the women criminals are found to be either non-earning or having income below 2000 per month which indicates that lower the income, higher the crime rate. Even those earning or employed are mostly found to be engaged in petty business undertaking or low grade employees. Therefore, appropriate vocational trainings, that is according to one's talent, interest and capability should be imparted while being lodged inside the prison and follow up training programme including employment opportunities should be made available.

As regards to preventive measures and rehabilitation, only in the month of August, 2007, some welfare schemes for the female inmates were jointly taken up by the Department of Women Development and Nagaland State Women's Commission in the form of setting up Vocational Training Centre for both District Jail, Kohima and Sub-Jail, Dimapur.

This programme aims to improve the quality of living for the inmates while helping them to take up some professional skill in order to make them earn their own living once they are freed from the prison. It can be said that if such programmes are manned by qualified and committed personnels, it would go a long way towards improving the living conditions of the women criminals in Nagaland. It can be suggested that while giving vocational training, proper counseling and career guidance should be imparted. If found necessary, financial aid to start small self-enterprise should be provided to deserving inmates.

REFERENCES

1. Ahuja, Ram; 2000; *Criminology*; New Delhi; Rawat Publications, p. 134.

2. Barnes; Harry Elmer and Negley K. Teeters; 1959; *New Horizons in Criminology;* New Delhi; Prentice Hall of India.

3. Darrow, Clarence; 1934; *Crime: Its Cause and Treatment;* London; Watts & Co.

4. *Nagaland Post,* Dated 04-05-03, 08-06-03, 22-02-04, 18-03-04, 28-10-04, 11-06-03

5. *Op. cit.,* Dated 17-04-05, *Sunday Post,* p. 8.

13

Women Empowerment through Self Help Groups in Nagaland

Elizabeth Vithazonu

> "You can tell the condition of a nation by looking at the status of its women"
>
> – *Jawaharlal Nehru*

Introduction

Empowerment is defined as the processes by which women take control and ownership of their lives through expansion of choices i.e. economic self-reliance, livelihood security, social mobilization and economic security.

The concept of women empowerment is the outcome of several important critiques and debates generated by the women's movement throughout the world particularly by the third world feminists. Its source can be traced from the interaction between feminism and the concept of "popular education" developed in Latin America in 1970's (Walters; 1991). The concept of women empowerment has its roots throughout the world in women movement.

"Becoming powerful" the literal meaning of the term" empowerment" is being used today in all spheres of life as a process to strengthen the elements of society. It is both a process and the result of the process, it is the transformation of the structures or institutions that reinforces and perpetuates gender discrimination. It is a process that enables women to gain access and control to material as well as information resources, gender disparity manifests itself in various forms, the most obvious being the trend of declining female ratio in population.

The 'empowerment' approach was first articulated in 1985 by Development Alternatives with women for a New Era (DAWN). This term received prominence in the early nineties in Western Countries. Women, the mother of mankind, has now become the subject of discussion with the growing and changing emphasis on the terms like women welfare, women development, women empowerment and gender equality in the social, economic and political analysis of both the developed and the developing countries. Empowering women contributes to social and economic development of the country. Therefore, in India the central government in its welfare programmes shifted the concept of development to empowerment in the Ninth Five Year Plan (1997-2001) and observed the year 2001 as "Women Empowerment Year". As women are essential for economic growth in the developing countries, no country can perhaps, eradicate poverty if it ignores women. Therefore, Planning Commission (1999-2000) had given specific emphasis on empowerment of women, and a new programme like Rural Women's Development and Empowerment Project (RWDEP) was introduced in states like UP, MP, Bihar, Haryana, Karnataka and Gujarat for a period of five years. The overall objective of the project is to enable empowerment of women by establishing self help groups which will improve the quality of their lives through greater access to and control over resources. The group-based model of self help is widely practiced for rural development, poverty alleviation and empowerment of women. It is an assisted self-help process which aims to mobilize people, give them a voice and build people.

A Brief History of Self Help Group (SHGs)

The concept of SHGs serves the principle "by the women, of the women and for the women". According to Morton the development of contemporary form of SHGs is generally ascribed to Alcoholic Anonymous, which was initiated in 1935 in the

USA (Morton and Shoden, 1994). The power of self help groups to help people suffering from other problems was not widely recognized until after World War II.

Self help groups have become very popular in South Asia and has emerged in order to help the rural poor, particularly women in securing inputs like credit and other services. The origin of SHG is from the Brain Child of Grammies Bank of Bangladesh, which was found by the economist, Prof. Mohammed Yunus of Chitagong University in the year 1975 and is now being followed in more than 53 developing countries including India. In India a number of NGO'S try Self Help Group approach to meet the credit challenges at Micro level in 1987-89 and NABARD took up the scheme on pilot project basis during 1991-1992 and took various initiatives to forge linkages of SHGs with Banks, but the concept became popular only when the Ninth Plan (1997-2002) has made its commitment to the objectives of "Empowering Women" as the agents of social change and development and remarkably Self Help Groups were considered to be one of the strategies to mark the beginning of major process of empowering women.

In Northeastern States the concept of SHG became popular only when Government of India introduced SGSY program in 1999 and visible progress has been seeing from the year 2000-01 onwards. With the exception of Assam all other States are still far behind in the implementation of this scheme as compared to other parts of India.

In the State of Nagaland the Movement of SHG became popular only after 2002 and many Government Departments and NGOs has been organizing Women SHGs at the grass root levels and promoting them credit linkages with banks and are also organizing various programmes and developmental skills to make them self-reliant. At present many women SHGs are seen as a major means for empowering women and are doing effectively. In recognition of the crucial role of women and their potential in the development process, the State Government of Nagaland has created the Directorate of Women Development during 2003-04 with the objective of uplifting women to function as equal partners and participants and the new directorate is implementing and initiating a number of welfare and development programmes for women.

The SHG can be the vehicle of economic empowerment by ensuring provision of training, employment and income-generation activities with the ultimate objective of making women economically independent. With economic independence, social empowerment can be created by more participation of women in public affairs and thereby facilitating affirmative development policies and programmes for development of women besides providing them easy and equal access to all basic minimum services so as to enable them to realize their full potential.

Self Help Group - Meaning

Self Help Groups as a catalyst agent for development at grass root level emerged in the principle of mutual help. It is an instrument of empowering people to work freely according to their mutual trust. It can be seen that the poor and the uneducated in the villages are incapacitated due to their social backwardness, illiteracy, low motivation and poor economic base. Besides, they lack access to the knowledge, information and opportunities which have become most important components of today's development process. Self Help Groups emerged to help rural poor and other incapacitated person in the villages.

A Self-Help Group (SHG) can be defined as a *"voluntary association of the people with a common goal of social and economic empowerment"*. It is a group of like-minded persons to maximize their individual and collective potentiality through collective effort.

It is a village based institution and is governed by certain rules and regulations, framed by the group members. People who are homogenous in terms of socio-economic background and traditional occupation come together for a common cause for the benefit of group members. Besides, it is a new programme for self-employment, skill development and skill up gradation improving productivity. SHGs are normally committed organizations which can bring sustainable development through the principles of empowerment of people. Generally, the weaker sections of society are empowered to take charge of their lives and their community and to design their future using all resources available to them.

The major objectives of SHGs are to save their income, avail the loan from the common fund of the group, create confidence and capabilities of the members, help the members by taking up of the social responsibilities to discuss the women related issues, dowry, health related like HIV/AIDS, etc.

The Major Features of SHGs are:

Homogeneous membership: As far as possible, the membership of a SHG may comprise of people from the same socio-economic background. Though difficult to define in clear terms, a major indicator of homogeneity in membership is absence of conflicting interests among members.

No discrimination: There should not be any kind of discrimination among members based on caste, religion or political affiliations.

Small membership: Ideally, the group size may be between 15 and 20, so that the members are able to participate in all activities of the SHG. In a smaller group, members get opportunity to speak openly and freely. However, the membership should not be too small.

Attendance: Total participation in regular group meetings lends strength to the effectiveness of SHGs. To achieve this, the SHGs should place strong emphasis on regular attendance in the group meetings.

Transparency in functioning: It is important that all financial and non-financial transactions are transparent in the functioning of the SHG. This promotes trust, mutual faith and confidence among its members.

Set of byelaws: The SHGs may discuss and finalize a set of byelaws indicating rules and regulations for the SHG's functioning and also chalk out roles and responsibilities of the members. It is better to have a written set of bylaws.

Thrift: The habit of thrift (small savings) is fundamental to the SHG's and helps in building up a strong common fund.

Utilizing savings for loaning: Once a SHG has accumulated a sizeable amount in the form of savings say for a period of about 3-6 months, the members may be allowed to avail loans against their savings for emergent consumption and supplementary income generating credit needs.

How to Organize SHG:

- There should be a clear cut goal for the formation of the group.
- Members of the group should be from the same locality.
- Every efforts should be made to form SHGs by the people of equal profession/status e.g. Weavers SHG, Artisans SHG, Farmers SHG etc.
- Every member of the group should be an earner.
- The members should be voluntary and not use any kind of compulsion.
- Members should have collective responsibilities.

Records to be maintained by the SHG:

- A copy of the Rules and Regulations of the group.
- Membership Register.
- Proceedings Minutes Book.
- Cash Book/Account Book.
- Pass Book for members.
- Loan Ledger.
- Others as required.

Success Stories of Women SHGs in Nagaland

In Nagaland Women SHGs has brought about changes in the field of social and economic status of women. Women members have been encouraged in decision making and sense of taking up responsibilities, belongingness and confidence in the male dominated society gatherings and meetings. Some successful stories of Women SHGs which proved that SHG can really empower women are mentioned below:

Vitso Women SHG – Secü Zubza

Vitso Women SHG was formed on 09/05/03 at Secü Zubza Village under Kohima District with 12 Women Members under the leadership of Smti. Keneiserienuo (who underwent training on 'Candle Making', sponsored by the S.S.B, Kohima Branch in the year 2002 at Sibsagar Assam) under the guidance of NCUI/ CEFP, Kohima. The main objective of the group was for socio-economic upliftment of its members. After formation of the SHG, the group got itself registered under the department of Industries and Commerce, Govt. of Nagaland with a permanent Industry registration No. 07/01239.

During the initial stages the group had a Monthly Thrift Collection of Rs.30/ head and was able to supplement it by marketing their local preparations such as Sticky Rice Roti, Pickles, and fermented Juice made out of Gooseberry, Wild apples, Agri and its allied products, etc. All their savings were than deposited at the NSCB Ltd. with these small savings, the group purchased a candle making machine and started their first production in the year 2004 and was introduced into the exhibition cum sale during the Hornbill Festival held at Kisama in 2004 Dec. Gradually the demand for their goods increased and seeing the success story of the SHG, the NSCB Ltd. sanctioned Rs. 10,000 as loan to the group to purchase a better candle making machine called the 'Iron Forma' in order to meet the market demand.

Today, the Group members are all versed in their activity and have started training other members in candle making. The group is now been well-established and they have started a small scale industry where work division has been introduced. The elderly members are engaged with the production while the younger members look after the distribution and sells and office management, etc. The group members have now started participating in the meetings, Seminars, Conference organized by different Govt. Dept. and NGOs. In the field of social development, the group organized programmes like HIV/AIDS

Awareness, Environment protection, Adult Education etc in collaboration with the concerned Department in the village.

Recently the groups have started vermiculture and are now planning to venture into floriculture. The members productivity and daily income has been increased to a great extend and as such an individual daily income has increased from Rs.20 to100 approximately. It is a fact that, Vitso Women SHG is marching towards attaining the goal for the socio-economic development of its members.

Dieze Women SHG - Jakhama

Dieze SHG was formed on 30th October 2003 with ten members under the National Co-operative Union of India, Cooperative Education Field Project, Kohima.

The group kick-started with a collection of Rs.50 every month for their fund and a get together was held once every month where they shared all their joys and sorrows. After some few months the group agreed to loan out their small savings to their members as productive and emergent credit needs at the interest rate of 3%.

Before the formation of the SHG, the members were only confined to their domestic works and agricultural fields. But after the formation of SHG in the year 2003, with great dedication and hard work the members under went different developmental trainings like, making woolen shoes, candles, jute bags and weaving. With their new acquired skills they have now started to supply their products to the Agri department, Kohima and woolen shoes to various hospitals in Kohima, these woolen shoes are even supplied to the Army Headquarters, Jakhama.

The SHG than opened their Group account at the NSCB Kohima and has also availed an amount of RS 15,000 as SHG loan which was repaid back to the Bank in the same year. After seeing their successful activities the Land Resources Department Project officer sanctioned Rs 10,000/- as seed money.

The Group purchased one fly shuttle machine (two group

members received training in weaving at Imphal) and has set up weaving units where various handloom products has been producing and sale it in and around Kohima. The groups are also engaged in potato cultivation which has a high local demand. The group is engaged in diversified economic activities and has started earning an average daily income of Rs. 150/- and as such their monthly contribution to the group fund has increased from Rs. 50 to Rs. 100.

What is worth mentioning about this group is that, they have been organizing various social awareness programmes such as awareness on HIV/AIDS, Family Planning and environmental protection in collaboration with various concerned departments in the village.

Financial Position of Dieze SHG till 30th June, 2008

1. Membership	-	10 members
2. Monthly deposit in the bank	-	Rs. 1000/-
3. Total Saving in the bank	-	Rs. 31,550/-
4. Loan to others	-	Rs. 25,500/-
5. Loan to members	-	Rs.24, 000/-
6. Loan from Bank	-	Nil
7. Percentage of recovery	-	100 %

Tsurhyu SHG – Wokha Village

The Tsurhyu Self Help Group was formed in Wokha Village with its Motto "Help to Rise". The group is to work for the welfare and upliftment of the rural poor, especially women sector. This group covers activities in Wokha Village, Humtso and Elumya villages.

In Lotha language *'Tsurhyu'* means women coming from different corners to form a group. Initially the groups were confused about SHG, but the members cooperated in all activities, later on a Government Officer briefly highlighted the concept of SHG. Since then the group has collected Rs. 50/- as a membership fee, than again Rs.100/- increased as for group fund. The group also conducted regular monthly meeting every 2nd Saturday to strengthen the group. Most of the group members are cultivators; only few are P.U. and Matriculate. Presently the group's fund has more than Rs. 1,00,0000/-. The present chairperson, Mrs. Mhonlumi Murry says, "Success does not come by luck but comes through the sincerity and dedication of the group members". Today the group's is looking for a plot of land in Wokha town to construct an RCC, Building for income generating purposes.

Activities

1. During the year 1999-2000 the group had cultivated ginger and potato and made a profit of Rs. 6020/-(Rupees six hundred twenty) only.
2. In the year 2000-2001 the group cultivated seasonal flowers and orchids and sold it to the market. Whereby the groups make an income of Rs. 5480/- (Rupees five thousand four hundred eight) only.
3. The group in 2002 sold printed calendars in the market and had a profit of Rs. 7560/- (Rupees seven thousand five hundred sixty) only.
4. In 2003 the group cultivated passion fruit (about 1.5 Hectares) and had income of Rs.8525/-(Rupees eight thousand five hundred twenty five) only as sale proceed.
5. In 2004, the group has planned to make the traditional method of making clay pot/ earthen pot for selling in the market.
6. Apart from the above mentioned activities the "SHG" is planning to take up a bigger project i.e. to buy a plot of land in Wokha Town and construct a building to generate income for their group.
7. Wokha being a big village it has many "SHG" numbering about 15. But due to lack of knowledge in running the "SHG" the groups has been facing many problems in its smooth functioning. Therefore, they are planning to organize a seminar on "SHG" to create "awareness programme" in 2004 with resource persons from outside.

Achievements

Out of the little saving they received in selling their products, the groups had taken up various activities in the rural areas (women sector) like Wokha village, Humtso Elumyo village and the response was quite satisfactory.

1. In the year 2002 the group had distributed milk, sugar, tealeaf to old aged people free of cost, and also assisted two poor children in getting admitted to school by way of giving cash assistance.
2. In 2003 the group distributed 5 kgs of rice each as a Christmas present to the widows of Wokha village.
3. In the year 2003 the group organized a seminar with a theme called "Child and Family Planning" and distributed medicines free of cost to the rural poor.

Another woman SHG from Tuensang district has also proved that SHG has lead to women empowerment in a big way. The group comprising of eight women formed a self help group in the far flung part of Tuensang district, initially started saving two to five rupees per month with an objective to buy a bus.

The SHG members who are mostly mothers had their own share of struggles and hardships for about a decade confronting their indifferent husbands and societal denial to materialize their far-fetched dream. The social sets up where they lived were costly and they thought their endeavor was against the social customs and practices' for womenfolk are believed to be confined only to family chores. Nevertheless, after enduring all the physical sufferings and psychological torture under such circumstances, this hard working women group achieved their dream which should be appreciated and admired.

The spirit of dignity of labour was found among these womenfolk who shied away the professional non-local potters by taking up works like unloading of heavy-laden trucks. They also took turns to weed each other fields and at times help the old and the widows. Thus, the SHGs, mostly women brought economic revelation in the area. Some of the income generating activities undertaken by them included selling of kerosene, rice, weaving products, agro-products, bee-farming and domestic needs besides many other businesses.

Today, women who had never had a single rupee are now finding difficult to handle thousands and lakhs of rupees. Their welfare work is highly appreciated and has gained recognition from the society. Through cash and kind, the groups support the poorest families in the village. Earlier their husbands shouldered the responsibility of the child's education, which with the passing of time and increase of group's income, the mothers have started assisting education expenses of the family. Every year the group disburses portion of the profit for school admission. All the eight members of the group have now admitted their children in urban private schools. Their patience and tolerance has paid as their husbands have started owning the groups activity as well as earning respect from the society. The group with support from ECS Edou Bank has dedicated the new 24 setter bus on March 25, 2008. This was truly a dream come true. Many in the area now look up at these women who have set a new trend for all to treasure (*Sunday Post* May, 4, 2008).

Conclusion

It is very clear from the above discussions that SHGs are the real tool for women empowerment in Nagaland. Self Help Groups have promoted and sharpened the entrepreneurial skills among women building self-confidence among the women members in the community. They are increasingly participating in decision making and community development activities like health, family and child welfare, AIDS awareness, sanitation programmes. Self Help Groups help women to achieve economic empowerment giving employment generation to the society; it increases the level of income and standard of living.

SHGs are changing the face of the countryside that is driven by poverty, illiterates and conservative ideas. SHGs has a great potential in creating awareness on day-to-day affairs, promoting saving habits, developing self and community assets, increasing the income level and increasing the social power and development. "All for all" the principle behind the concept of Self Help Groups generates self confidence, self security and self-reliance.

The strength of the women gets multiplied and even irresistible when they organize the Self Help Groups into clusters within an area and go on to form a federation of SHGs. SHGs are fast emerging as "Women Movement" throughout the nation and their activism has influenced the policy and planning of the government for the empowerment and development.

The activities of the SHGs are not limited. There are multiple activities which can be taken up by the SHGs. The SHGs have many advantages like micro finance, low or no transaction costs, low or no default rate, value added services, etc. SHGs are a very important component especially in Nagaland as they are good in self-employment activities and their need depends on micro-funding. With better coordination the structuring and functioning of SHGs can be enhanced.

> *"The best thermometer to the progress of a nation is its treatment of its women".*
>
> \- Swami Vivekananda

REFERENCES

1. NABARD; *A Handbook on Forming Self Help Groups (SHGs)*; pp. 1-23.
2. National Cooperative Union of India; *The Cooperator*; Vol. 42, No. 4 October 2004, Vol. 45, No. 4, October 2007, Vol. 45, No. 7, January 2008.
3. Suguna, B; 2006; *Empowerment of Rural Women through Self-Help Groups*; New Delhi; Discovery Publishing House.
4. Srivastava, Alka; 2005; *Self Help Groups and Civil Society: A Preliminary Study*.
5. Misra, Kamal K & Janet Huber Lowry (ed.); 2007; *Recent Studies on Indian Women - Empirical Work of Social Scientists*; Jaipur; Rawat Publication.
6. Singh, S.K & S.P. Pandey; 2007; *Empowerment of Scheduled Caste Women through Self Help Groups*; New Delhi, Serials Publications.

14

Naga Women and Political Participation: *An Overview*

Viraho Hibo

The Nagas belong to the patrilineal society which obviously follows the patriarchal type of authority. It also means that, power and decision-making remains the domain of the men folks. In the past, this pattern was augmented by the head hunting practice of our fore-fathers. The role of men was mostly confined to the concept of 'protection'. Social changes occurred and re-occurred: education, Christianity, westernization, modernisation and others became the main vehicles of change. Many traditional statuses, roles and practices too had changed: some for the better, some for the worst. But one aspect of the society which is resisting change is the non-active political participation of women or the resistance to involve women in the decision-making processes. The resistance rests in the mind-set of both men and women, though the men folks are visibly stronger over this gender issue.

Traditional Form of Governance

The traditional Naga society engendered the role of women to house-hold chores, taking care of children, being a docile wife to their husbands besides working in the field. Women were in no way involved in the policy making or in any decision-making bodies. Leadership and decision-making was the prerogative of the male members. In every Naga village, social groups were divided into families, clans, *Khels* and others. In every *Khel*, some male members were assigned to look after the administration of the village and settle disputes. The political infrastructure from the *'Khel'* moves to the village level where the village councils draws its powers and responsibilities from the people, through their support and consensus drawn from tradition. This form of village governance was the practice in majority of the villages with exception to some village chiefs, hereditary or elected and also Anghs who were the traditional kings amongst the Konyak Nagas.

Women in National and State Politics

State elections in Nagaland began in 1964 and since then, less than 20 women have contested in it. None of the women candidates have ever won. There has not been a single woman member in the State Legislative Assembly either by straight contest, bye-polls or nomination. There is also no reservation for women in the State Legislative Assembly too. The only woman who made a notable entry into politics was Rano Shaiza who was the first and only lady from Nagaland to become Member of Parliament (MP) when she was elected to the 6th Lok Sabha.

Thus, when one looks at the National and State political scenario, women still has a long way to catch-up with the mainstream politics which is again dominated by men. The 33% reservation issue becomes plausible when one studies the ground realities of the plight of women in politics.

Local and Municipal Bodies

In Nagaland, instead of Panchayati Raj system, Nagaland Village and Area Councils, 1975 was enacted for self-governance at the village levels. However, the Nagaland Municipal Act, 2001 delegates' urban governance to elected representatives of the towns. The Act has three categories of urban bodies. Accordingly; there are three Town Municipal councils namely, Kohima, Dimapur and Mokokchung. There are also 16 Town Committees and Urban Station Committees. These Councils and Committees are given the responsibility of developing and maintaining the basic amenities and general infrastructure of their respective towns.

Apparently in this area too, women have basically very less involvement. In relation to this issue, the Nagaland State Assembly in keeping with Article 371(A) of the Constitution of India had passed the Nagaland Municipal (Amendment) Act 2006 whereby 33% of seats in the civic bodies were reserved for women and the same was notified (The Morung Express, Vol. III issue 230). When the government of Nagaland decided to implement 33% reservation for women in Mokokchung Municipal elections, there was a hue and cry raised by the men folks saying that it is against customary laws. In reaction to this, the various women bodies, led by the Nagaland State Women Commission met the State governing bodies. A bandh was also called by the 'All Wards Union Mokokchung Town' on September 4th, 2008 in protest against the 33% women reservation in the ensuing Mokokchung Municipal Council elections.

Village Councils

The Nagaland Village and Area Councils Act, 1978 was enacted to empower the traditional village institutions and village courts guided by the customary law in order to make the maximum utilisation of governing bodies existing at that point of time. Under this Act, no women were included as the council members were chosen using customary practices by the village male elders, village chiefs and Anghs. The Village Councils are vested with full power and authority to deal with all internal administration of the village. They also act as village courts with both civil and judicial duties and have the power to maintain law and order within the village jurisdiction.

In the villages, customary laws are used instead of modern laws. In this set-up, women have no status, no role, no voice nor representations in any manner. The Village Councils are especially strong as they have the back-up of the Government too.

Village Development Boards

The Village Development Board (VDB) is the first significant body to include women in any decision-making process though many women representatives are struggling to make their voices heard in the sea of the patrilineal ethos. It is for this reason that VDB will be dealt extensively in this presentation. The concept of 'Village Development Board' is a very unique experience ever introduced throughout the State of Nagaland. In its essence, it means giving power to the people to plan developmental schemes for themselves, which is commonly called grass-root planning. This is in clear contrast with central planning that the country after Independence has been following initially. After several decades it was found that centralised planning was not really in touch with the grass-root level of society and their reality. In fact, many plans have been responsible only in widening the gap between the rich and the poor. Therefore; an experiment was made even in Nagaland called the 'Village Development Board'.

Origin of VDB

The spirit of socialism had a strong base in the state of Maharashtra and Gujarat in the early days of the post Independent India. It was, therefore, the idea of those idealistic socialist leaders who propagated the need to share the wealth of the state equally between the rich and the poor. In order to achieve this, some fundamental grass-root planning which resembled the existing VDB type of schemes were tried out in other parts of the country. The experiment could not succeed because the recipient villagers were too thinly spread out. It is for these reasons that this brilliant idea failed to strike root both in Maharashtra and Gujarat. However, a significant turn was felt in Nagaland when A.M. Gokhale, an I.A.S. Officer, was posted to Phek District as its Deputy Commissioner. Being the son of the famous socialist Leader S.M. Gokhale, he began to toy with the idea of introducing the failed experiment of Maharashtra and Gujarat in Phek District of Nagaland. He was positive that the idea of a village developing its own needs and requirements will surely prove to be effective. He was also encouraged by the close social setting of the people within a compact ecological spread. He also studied as to why the generous funds that were doled out to the state were not percolating down to the villages in particular. He realized the representatives of the people could only make faint noises in the newspapers, that also rarely, but it was to no effect too. He also noticed that elections come and go but nothing happens much for the good of the people in spite of many rich developmental promises.

In this context, A.M. Gokhale realized the crux of the problem and tried to devise a system in such a way that various funds being allotted will go directly to the people to be planned and utilised according to the local needs. This also disallows the funds meant for the villagers to be exercised by high government officials at their own discretion. This was how V.D.B. took its root in Nagaland. He also formulated a model draft and a model rule which was circulated to a select group of officers to draw useful critical appraisal on the basis of which he could finally distil the idea and after securing the approval of the state cabinet, the V.D.B. took its foundation. Phek District was the first test pilot area for VDB in action. It actually started at Ketsapomi Village in October, 1976. After a year of implementing the VDB schemes throughout Phek District, it showed phenomenal positive results. VDB scheme became an instant success which prompted the State Government to adopt the VDB throughout the State of Nagaland. In gradual progression, according to positive results shown, VDB allocation of fund per house-hold was raised from Rs.100/- to Rs. 200/- to Rs. 750/- to Rs. 800/-, out of which 25% is earmarked for women activities and 20% is earmarked for youth activities. There are 1086 number of VDBs existing in Nagaland. The topic of VDB, of late, is not a very open subject as there have been cases of misappropriation, infiltration of party politics and bureaucratic influence within the VDB and its functionaries. Despite these drawbacks, the VDB concept is still recognised to be the main democratic process of grass-root planning.

There are two main sources of funds for the VDBs. (i). Matching grant schemes: the Government's contribution to the villagers common fund is equal to the amount of the common fund raised by the villages which are invested for a minimum of 5 years in fixed deposit accounts in the banks followed by continuous re-investments. (ii) Grant-in-aid: The department of rural development in Nagaland allots part of the state Government's annual plan fund village wise instead of sector wise allotment as is the common practice in other state of India. This ensures recurring source of funds to the villages. (iii) The VDBs source of income is also through centrally sponsored funds like Integrated Rural Development Programme (IRDP), State Rural Development Agency (SRDA) also implements IRDP and allied programmes. The VDBs are recognised as its field agencies and subsidy amount is directly released for the same. Consequently rural development department also includes schemes for women.

Women's Schemes

In 1984-85, 25% of the grant-in-aid was decided to earmark for women development programmes, and thus far, that same percentage of VDBs incoming funds are reserved for women. Population wise, women are no lesser but the socio-structural pattern with all the age-old practices of the patriarchal system stands in the way of involving women at any decision-making bodies even at the grass-root level.

Field Study of VDB

In order to study the VDB and the role of Angami women, five villages from Southern Angami area were chosen to be the universe of the research. The villages chosen were namely Khuzama, Viswema, Jakhama, Kigwema and Phesama. These highway villages were chosen because they represent villages which are supposed to be on the verge of undergoing the process of social change towards modernisation. Both Observation and Interview method were employed for the purpose of data collection. Data collection involved both the genders. Some past and present VDB functionaries were interviewed which included both men and women, but more emphasis was given to the female respondents. Other village members were also interviewed using the technique of Simple random sampling where the persons met at the place of study, irrespective of gender or qualification.

It was found out that all the villages studied had one woman representative to the mainstream VDB but plays no active role in it. At best she is called for attending meetings at times and asked to give her signature for official related papers. If not for that the planning and management of VDB funds are managed separately. The mainstream VDB secretary gets Rs.1000/- as remuneration whereas the women VDB secretary gets no remuneration. She acts, in most villages, as the go- between, between the women society and the mainstream VDB. The study also showed that most of the women VDB funds are planned and managed by the Women Society of the village. The women folks are utilising their 25% funds for managing projects like rice mills, weaving units and building community houses after community houses, with not much idea and scope to invest in other areas. Most of them when asked about their future plans in managing the VDB funds said they will build more buildings. In fact, many of them had already expanded their building projects to towns like Kohima. There are no plans involving the socio-economic upliftment of the individual woman. In fact, all the respondents answered negatively when asked whether any plans are included to lift up the status and welfare of the individual poor woman. Such plans are yet to be included in the horizon of women VDBs at the grass-root level.

The findings of the field- work turn out be quite revealing of the status of Angami women both at the traditional and the modern institutions. The Angami followed the patriarchal system, from time immemorial, therefore the traditional socio- economic structures firmly followed likewise too. The VDB concept suited the structural and the functional aspect of the clustered villagers. But there was no adequate provision laid to unconditionally include the women folks even in a modern governmental institution such as the VDB. This simple step which has not been included at the initial stages of the VDB is now responsible for creating a huge gap leading to irreparable gender division at the grass-root levels. The ability to voice out concerns and suggestions at the mainstream VDB by the women is negligible. It was seen only in one instance where an educated woman VDB representative could freely plan and give her suggestions sitting among the other male members. When asked whether developmental works can be done together with the men folks, which will also prevent slicing of the developmental funds into piece-meal manner, most of the women respondents, including the women VDB secretaries were reluctant to the idea. They expressed their view that if they are to be clubbed together with the mainstream VDB in the present situation, they are apprehensive that they may get deleted completely instead of taking part in the planning and development of the village. At the same time, they feel that they are also capable of involving actively in the development processes even at the mainstream VDB. Some even suggested that the men folks are not planning and using the funds wisely and judiciously. This expression was augmented by the fact that the study also revealed that there were more misappropriations of funds and misunderstandings among the mainstream VDB which is operated by men as compared to the women's 25% fund management. The records of the women VDBs were also more meticulously maintained as compared to the mainstream VDB.

Road-Map for involving Women at the Policy and Decision-Making Level

The Naga ethnic identity and the patrilineal system of life, be it inheritance of ancestral property or land strictures and so on must be adequately guarded but certain things which can benefit society must be adapted with the changing times. Women constitute more than half of the Naga population. And when this sizeable portion of the population is disregarded in the decision-making bodies, the concerned population's needs and requirements will never be seriously known and considered. The concept of VDB is to let people plan for themselves and develop themselves because they know themselves best. Women are a part of that 'people' and when they are excluded the picture is not complete. Majority of the Naga villages still keeps a safe distance from women at the actual practice of VDB related decision-making level. This practice may not really be beneficial at the broader village level. Women without men will be handicapped to a great extent, the same stands for men too.

When the womenfolk's receives their shares, money is collected, accumulated and sometimes common buildings exclusively for women are built or some other exclusive programs are made for women only. Many of the respondents when asked about future plans said they have no idea. This brings a gap and questions the VDB system of gender division. Men and women are different in many ways but they are also complimentary and supplementary to each other, as such when there are too many great divisions, it may hamper socio-economic developments. Both men and women must acknowledge that they differ in sexual attributes and so many other differentiations exists but also should recognise that thought patterns and action plans must be contributory from both ends. Man lives within societies comprising of both the sexes, therefore participation of both men and women shall surely win positive rewards.

Nagas from time immemorial had been following the patrilineal/patriarchal system of governance. In this context it is not men who are refusing to admit women at the decision-making bodies but it is the traditional way of life that is still taking time to shift to modern concepts of accommodating women even in a modern and recent construction like the VDB. Many a time, women themselves feel it is inappropriate to be part of the bodies that plans and does the decision-making, especially at the village level, not knowing that they are making their daughters go a few more years backward which in turn will have a very negative impact on the overall societal progress towards positive changes. There are certain concerns in this regard and rays of hope because it involves the Government too. A few suggestions can be given:

1. Create VDB bodies where any gender will not have feelings of being left-out or develop feelings of belonging to a minority group. VDB is a decision-making body to develop the village, thus every problem or scope of development must be studied and planned together by both men and women. Reservation of seats leads to discriminations. The Government must not create gender division by giving reservations to either male or female. It must frame rules and regulations in such a manner

that the entire population be adequately represented. No sex should dominate, no clan should dominate, and no individual should dominate. It should be a body that has a sample to represent the whole population.

2. In majority of the Naga villages, one can find a good number of literate women. The practice of not involving women in decision- making bodies' maybe lessened if educated women members at the proper VDB are involved initially, in order to take away the psychological barrier created due to the age-old customs and traditions.

3. The Government should facilitate programmes to accommodate both the sexes together in order to avoid further gender division and place both negative and positive sanctions to ensure that its directives are carried out effectively. Naga men are sensible and therefore if it is justifiable it will be surely supported.

4. VDB funds can be used judiciously for concrete developmental works and not just spent on wrestling events, hosting of Jubilees etc. It would be a much better idea to invest in higher education.

5. If water systems, proper drainages and other sanitary projects are included from the VDB fund then a lot of health related issues which comes through unhygienic surroundings may be averted. Such suggestions and pressures may come more strongly from the women folks. These issues which require constant developmental approaches for improvements and which are also the domains of women where constructive planning and suggestions may be given by them.

6. Education of the girl child must be given special emphasis because it is the most effective tool to liberate traditional strictures. Even males must be encouraged seriously to pursue liberal education because it can make one less conservative. It will help one to recognise quality rather than pre-conceived notions of status based on gender. It is a known fact that families and societies which had

the opportunity of being properly educated with quality education are more open to gender related issues and of rectification, if any. So also men who had educated wives and educated daughters have no problems on questions of equity.

7. When it comes to village created common funds, the women folks constitute half of the workforce. No special consideration is used to exempt them from manual works but when fund from various sources comes they are singled out and given 25% Share which is a little irrational, if one is to be logical. Therefore, participation and inclusion must be balanced so that any gender does not suffer at the status scale.

8. It will do well for the Nagas in general if the VDBs fully make use of the various funds allotted to the villages for actual developmental works. The future generation's plight of overall societal status and development will depend on how visionary we have been in utilising our village funds. Therefore, long term plans should be adopted to take full advantage of the given opportunity.

Conclusion

Against the backdrop given, an analysis of Naga women and politics can be arrived at some conclusions. The political participation of Naga women is still in its nascent stage. It can be seen from experiences and Government modules that the past policy makers consciously or unconsciously planned all decision-making processes and bodies, strictly following the patriarchal system of the Naga society. The customary laws at times clashes with modern laws. It is a fact that Nagas are in the process of change. Many aspects of the Naga ways of living has changed, many new social norms have replaced most of the age-old practices but when it comes to political participation; Naga women are still lagging very far behind. In comparison to the degrees of changed felt in most aspects of life, involving women in the decision-making process is the slowest to pick up the winds of change. There is also a visible sign that in the Naga society, there are instances of pre-modern, modern and post-modern attitudes co-existing with each other. It is observed that there is also a clash between modernity and tradition especially with regards to the changing gender roles and the need for adaptation to new roles. The patrilineal system can help save and preserve the tribal identity of the Nagas in respect to their land, culture and others but if a balance is not maintained to accommodate the forces of change, gender alienation can easily arise to bring about dissension within the society. The Complimentary peaceful co-existence of both the genders should be sought in all aspects of life for a society to move towards wholesome progressive development. Pre-modern, modern and post-modern ideals and practices must be carefully analysed and policies be made to suit the changing times without obvious discrimination to any type of gender.

REFERENCES

1. Abdul, B. *et. al.*, (ed.); 1979; *Rural Development in South East Asia.* New Delhi; Vikas Publishing House Pvt. Ltd.
2. Ao, L.A; 1993; *Rural Development in Nagaland*; New Delhi; Har-Anand Publications.
3. Bhatnagar, S. & S.S. Chid; 1987; *Rural Development in India: A Strategy for Socio Economic Change*; New Delhi; Ess Ess Pub.
4. Bordoloi, R.C. & C. Shankarih; 1981; 'Extension Education and Rural Development', in *International Experience in Communication and Innovation*; Vol.-I, New York; John Wiley and Sons.
5. Dagar, Rainuka (ed.); 1998; *Manual on Women's Development and Gender Justice*; Institute for Development and Communication (IDC); Chandigarh.
6. Deb, P.C. (et. al.); 1979; *Integrated Rural Development Programmes: A Case Study in Punjab*; Draft sixth five year plan; Government of India.
7. D' Souza, Alphonsus & Christina Kekhrieseno; 2002; *Coping with Social Change in North-East India: A Comparative Study of Three Ethnic Groups in North-East India (Aka, Angami and Dimasa)*; St. Joseph's College, Jakhama, Nagaland.
8. Ghanshyam, S & H.R. Chaturvedi; 1983; *Gandhian Approach to Rural Development*; Delhi; Ajantsa Pub.

9. Gokhale, A.M; 1984; *The Common Fund Programme: A Strategy for Alleviating Rural Poverty in Nagaland.*

10. Hibo, Visakhonu; 1992; *Social Change and the Angami Nagas;* St. Mary's College, Shillong, Meghalaya.

11. Liegise, Buno; 2006; *The Struggle of Rural Women and Winds of Change in Nagaland;* Hudi Dielie; Angami Students Union, Issue no. I.

12. Madam, G.R; 1983; *Village Development in India;* Delhi; Allied Pub.

13. Pillai, Jaya Kothai; 1995; *Women and Empowerment;* New Delhi; Gyan Publishing House.

14. Rao, Digumarti Bhaskara (et. al.); 2000; *Status and Advancement of Women;* New Delhi; A.P.H. Pub.

15. Roy, Aphuno Chase; 2004; *Women in Transition: Angami Naga Women from 1878 to the Present;* Published by the Author.

16. Singh, R.B; 1987; *Planning for Rural Development;* New Delhi; Discovery Pub.

17. Zehol, Lucy; 1998; *Women in Naga Society;* New Delhi; Regency Publications.

18. ESO-02; 1990; *Women and Society,* Indira Gandhi National Open University; New Delhi.

19. State Institute of Rural Development (SIRD); 1999; Training of the Members of Village Councils & Village Development Boards (VDBs).

20. The Morung Express, Vol. III, Issue 230 & 245, Dimapur, 2008.

Index

***